CITY BY THE SEA

Jn R Moon

December, 2010

A plan of Ancient Falmouth, embracing the tract from the Spurwink River to North Yarmouth, with the location of the original settlers.

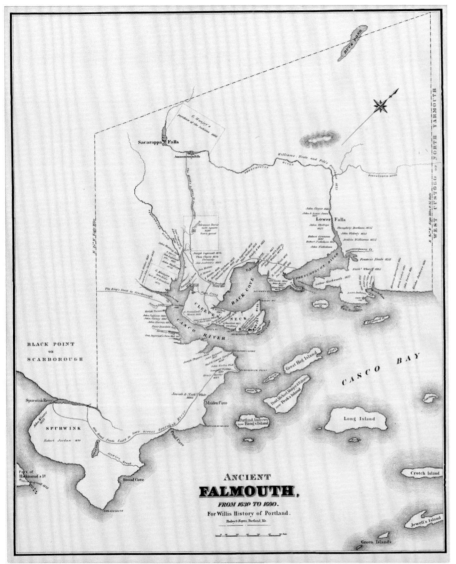

This remarkable map occurred as an illustration on page 94 of William Willis's landmark *History of Portland from 1632 to 1864*, published in 1865 by Bailey & Noyes at 82 Exchange Street. The period the map covers, 1630 to 1690, was an era characterized by, as historian William David Barry best put it, "grinding poverty, guerilla warfare, and unending litigation." Notice that "Ancient Falmouth" comprised the present day towns of Portland, South Portland, Cape Elizabeth, Westbrook and Falmouth. How did this come to be? A charter for the Plymouth Company that had originally been issued by King James I in 1606, giving exclusive rights to specified individuals to develop and exploit lands taken in the name of the English crown, was re-issued in 1620 to the reorganized Plymouth Company. In 1622, the reorganized Plymouth Council for New England, as it was then known, granted land patents to Sir Fernando Gorges, the original proprietor of Maine. All grants in Ancient Falmouth stem from land granted to Gorges, including that of Arthur Mackworth in Falmouth Foreside, George Cleeve and Richard Tucker on Falmouth Neck and Trelawney-Goodyear in Cape Elizabeth. But relying of the largess of any king was risky business. In 1625, Charles I became the new king. The first thing he did was rescind the 1620 charter, while issuing a new one with a new cast of characters, creating much contentiousness and "unending litigation" among settlers. Land ownership problems continued to cause confusion and distress, and an organized, elected government was needed. Gorges, meanwhile, had died destitute in England in 1647 without achieving his colonial aspirations. The Massachusetts Bay Colony, under a new charter, then acquired jurisdiction over the province of Maine, the grant area formerly controlled by the Gorges group. Finally, in 1658 the General Court of Massachusetts assumed control over all the grants and, in the following edict, created a new town named Falmouth: *"Those places formerly called Spurwink and Casco Bay, from the east side of the Spurwink River to the Clapboard Islands in Casco Bay, shall run back eight miles into the country, and henceforth shall be called Falmouth."* The name Falmouth was derived from the ancient Cornwall town at the mouth of the Fal River in England, whence came several early English settlers. Though formed in 1658, Falmouth was not incorporated until 1718. The first town to separate from Ancient Falmouth was Cape Elizabeth/South Portland in 1776; Falmouth Neck became the small town of Portland in 1786, Westbrook/Deering broke away in 1814 (known initially as Stroudwater, then changed to Westbrook after Col. Thomas Westbrook, the mast agent); in 1871 the town of Deering broke off from Westbrook and became its own town for 28 years; in 1895 South Portland broke off from Cape Elizabeth and became its own town; and finally in 1899 the town of Deering was annexed to the City of Portland. Now you know.

CITY BY THE SEA

A Photographic History of Portland, Maine

BY
John R. Moon

Author's Note

This book has not been edited to adhere to the Chicago Manual of Style Standards.
Upon Stephen King's advice, however, I have read *The Elements of Style*, by William Strunk Jr. and E.B. White.
I think the result here is a book that is highly readable. Still, there are bound to be at least a few typographical errors
remaining that I have failed to detect, spell checker or no.. For that, I beg the reader's indulgence.

Library of Congress Control Number: 2010933172

Published by Elysium Press
PO Box 66747
Falmouth, ME 04105

Printed in the United States of America by Penmor Lithographers, Lewiston, Maine.

On the front cover: The J.B. Brown Memorial Building was built on Congress Street in Portland in 1882-83 by sons Philip Henry Brown and John Marshall Brown to honor their father, John Bundy Brown, who had died in 1881 when he sustained a concussion from a fall at his private estate – Bramhall - on the Western Promenade. For years, the J.B. Brown Building was home to the Rines Brothers Company which, in a daring move, relocated from their Middle Street store to this stunning block on Congress Street. An exquisite example of the Queen Anne style, the building was designed by a young John Calvin Stevens while working with the Fassett firm (for more on John Calvin Stevens, see Appendix M on page 187). The photograph dates from 1912 and shows the apparel people wore at that time. Note especially that everyone in the picture is wearing a hat. For more on this building and photograph, see pages 14-15.

On the back cover: The same block as it appears today. The Rines Brothers Company lasted here at this location until the 1970s, when malls became the rage. Today the building is in the middle of Portland's newly-designated Arts District, and is home to a variety of art galleries.

Contents

This Book is Dedicated to Norman Hull Morse

Two early views of Monument Square. The one on the left was taken in the 1890's, shortly after the building of the Soldiers and Sailors Monument of 1891. An electric trolley is making its way up Congress Street, and horse-drawn carriages can still be seen moving people across town. There are no cars. The end of an era was rapidly approaching, as steel frame construction and the introduction of elevators would soon make "skyscrapers", like those shown on the right, possible. The image on the right shows Monument Square around 1950, when Portland reached it highest population of about 77,000, thanks in large measure to the 30,000 jobs created during World War II making Liberty ships in the shipyards across the Fore River. Both the Fidelity Building of 1909-10 and the Chapman Building of 1924 are visible, along with many automobiles making their way around the monument, before the square was turned into a pedestrian-friendly walkway.

Acknowledgements

My thanks to everyone who assisted with the research and writing of this book.

I am particularly indebted to Earle G. Shettleworth, Jr. and his staff at the Maine Historic Preservation Commission for supplying so many of the vintage images that make this book special. Thanks also to Earle for reading the manuscript and sharing with me his encyclopedic knowledge of Portland. The citizens of Maine are indeed fortunate to have him and his organization as a resource.

I also wish to thank the staff of the Maine Historical Society for supplying many of the images in this book from among the Society's vast collection. Jamie Rice, Dani Fazio and Bill Barry were, as always, a pleasure to work with and of invaluable assistance with making this book less difficult to put together than it might otherwise have been.

Writing a book of nonfiction requires help from a lot of people, both in the research phase and during the actual production process itself. In this regard, I wish to thank the following individuals, groups and organizations, without whose assistance this book might never have seen the light of day: The Children's Museum of Maine, Toby Crockett of Greater Portland Landmarks; friends of the Falmouth Historical Society; Peter Gribbin of Portland High School; Jim Iacono of Maine Aviation; Mr. Peter Lekousi; Maine Medical Center; Ms. Catherine Michaels; Bill Needleman of the City of Portland; Leah Osberg; Ruth Porter of L.L. Bean; Ann Reagan of the Inn at St. John; Mr. Howard C. Reiche, Jr.; Mr. and Mrs. James and Jennifer Rice; Abraham Schecter, curator of special collections, Portland Public Library; the Thomas Memorial Library, City of Cape Elizabeth; Sherrin Vail of Avesta Housing; the Westbrook Historical Society; and Leann Wiley of the Portland Museum of Art.

Books that I found useful for researching this volume include the following: William Willis, *The History of Portland* (1865); Augustus F. Moulton, *Portland by the Sea* (1926); Edward H. Elwell, *Portland and Vicinity* (1881); Greater Portland Landmarks, *Portland* (1972); William Goold, *Portland in the Past* (1886); William David Barry and Francis W. Peabody, *Tate House, Crown of the Mast Trade* (1982); Earle G. Shettleworth, Jr. and William David Barry, *Mr. Goodhue Remembers Portland, Scenes from Mid-19th Century* (1981); Peter E. Gribbin, *A History of Portland High School, 1821 through 1981* (1982); Howard C. Reiche, Jr., *Closeness, Memories of Mrs. Munjoy's Hill* (2002); Joyce K. Bibber and Earle G. Shettleworth Jr., *Portland* (2007); Frederick L. Thompson, *The Rines Family Legacy* (2005); William Levinsky, *A Short History of Portland* (2007); Joseph A. Conforti, *Creating Portland, History and Place in Northern New England* (2005); and James P. Baxter, *Christopher Levett of York, The Pioneer Colonist in Casco Bay* (1893). In total, the author has read more than 10,000 pages from these books as an aid to preparing insightful captions for this book. I can only hope that my efforts will prove satisfying to the reader.

For his steadfast support for this project, and for believing in it when few others did, a heartfelt thanks is due to Mr. Norman Hull Morse, to whom this book is dedicated. For helping me claw my way back to life after a near fatal small bowel surgery this year, and for giving me the courage to complete this book, a special debt of gratitude is owed to nurse Cathy Prokey. She is a credit to her profession, and a true angel on earth.

Unless otherwise noted, all contemporary images in this book were photographed by the author.

Often I think of the beautiful town

That is seated by the sea;

Often in thought go up and down

The pleasant streets of that dear old town,

And my youth comes back to me.

>   Henry Wadsworth Longfellow,
>   *My Lost Youth*

The year is 1928, and two boys play with an Air Mail wagon in their East End neighborhood along Washington Avenue at the foot of Munjoy Hill. Then, as now, Portland has always been a great place to raise children.

Introduction

Portland is a small but very cosmopolitan city situated on the southern coast of Maine at Casco Bay. It has a gallant past.

The fall of the Roman Empire may seem a strange place to start a book about the history of Portland, which any third grade student from the Nathan Clifford Elementary School can tell you was settled in 1632 by a man named George Cleeve. But every story has to start somewhere, and ours begins here. My thesis, by no means original, is that it was the fall of the empire (particularly in the east) and subsequent closure of trade routes to the Orient that gave Europeans an incentive to explore the West, including the coast of Maine, for a possible sea route to India. To understand the reasons why an English adventurer like George Cleeve risked his life to sail half way around the world and settle in a cold, barren remote wilderness, one has to step back a little to view the forest instead of the trees. This requires a brief review of world history, and the antecedent conditions that made such a voyage possible, perhaps even inevitable. So indulge me, for a moment, for a quick detour through time. The journey will be brief but worthwhile.

The first date of importance is September 4th, 476, when the 16-year-old Romulus Augustulus abdicated imperial office and returned to the Gulf of Naples with a pension. Though he was the last of the Roman emperors, historians do not even bother to record when he died. It was Odacer, leader of a tribe of Germanic mercenaries, who now became King of Italy. Gaul was in the hands of the Visigoths, the Vandals controlled North Africa, and Roman Britain was well en route to becoming Anglo-Saxon England. The empire of Rome in the west survived now only as a memory. *In the East*, however, emperors continued to rule for another thousand years, until the fall of Constantinople in 1453. It was in that year that the Sultan Mehmet the Conqueror and his vast Ottoman army arrived outside the walls and laid siege to the city. Eventually the great ramparts were breached and the Ottoman troops poured into Constantinople. During the three days of massacre that followed, the head of the last Byzantine emperor Constantine IX Paleologus was severed from his body with a scimitar and placed on a column amidst jeering crowds in the Hippodrome. The empire was now officially dead.

Around this time a new idea began to take hold which would ultimately lead to settlements in the New World, including one in Portland. Could it be possible that the Atlantic Ocean was the shortest road to the spice regions of the Orient – a shorter road, that is, than the overland passage normally taken by merchants? Such a route was now necessary because parts of the overland route to India had been closed to Europeans after the Turks captured Constantinople. Paulo Toscanelli (1397-1482), the great Italian mathematician and astronomer, appears to have been the first person in history to entertain the idea of sailing west in order to reach India. He eventually convinced a high-strung Genoese sea captain named Christopher Columbus to try it, and on August 3, 1492 his tiny fleet of three ships set sail from Cape Palos, near Cartagena, in the hour before dawn. The rest, of course, is history.

Others followed in Columbus's wake, but as William Willis tells us, "In the beginning of the year 1603, there was not one European family on the whole coast of America, from Florida to Greenland. The entire coast was now open to European enterprise." In 1606, King James I of England granted a charter founding the Virginia Company. It had two parts. The Plymouth Company was to establish settlements from the Hudson River north, and the London Company was given land from the Hudson River south. In 1607, the Plymouth Company established Popham Colony, which lasted less than two years, and the London Company established the Jamestown Colony, which had a desperate time but managed to survive. It started exploration of its own and in 1610 began sending fishing vessels to the Gulf of Maine. The earliest movement for settlement of the area, however, did not begin until Captain John Smith visited the Maine coast in 1614.

Introduction

After returning to England he wrote his *Description of New England,* which encouraged Englishmen to settle in Maine, but he himself never returned.

In 1622, the reorganized Plymouth Council for New England granted land patents to Sir Fernando Gorges and John Mason. Through an agreement with Mason, Gorges received the territory in Maine. The following year, Christopher Levett was granted six thousand acres and, accompanied by a small group of men, settled on an island in Casco Bay, probably the present House Island (see page 323). He remained only a short time before returning back to England to recruit others to come back with him. Unfortunately, he never made it. He died in 1630, the crew he left behind on House Island deserted, and the settlement was never heard from again. In 1628 a trader named Walter Bagnall arrived on nearby Richmond Island and set up a trading post dealing in furs and fish. After cheating the local Indians for three years, in 1631 the Indians got even by murdering Bagnall. That brings us down to George Cleeve.

Cleeve had settled on Richmond Island with his wife Joan, daughter Elizabeth, and servant Oliver Weeks. Along with a partner, Richard Tucker, he established a prosperous farming and trading business there. In 1632, a man named John Winter arrived, representing Robert Trelawney and Moses Goodyear, who had been granted a tract of land that included the area occupied by Cleeve. Cleeve and Tucker were ordered to leave, so they loaded their boat with Cleeve's family, his servant, and their personal belongings, and sailed toward Casco Bay and the peninsula. They found a suitable spot next to the present Fore and Hancock Streets and became the first white settlers of Portland. Luckily, for posterity, Cleeve returned to England in 1637 to formally secure his property on the Neck. He went to Fernando Gorges and for one hundred pounds sterling received a two-thousand year lease. All property rights in present day Portland stem from this lease. Gorges died destitute in 1647, never having achieved his colonial aspirations. Finally, in 1658, the General Court of Massachusetts assumed control over all the grants and created a town called Falmouth, known today as Portland.

Architecturally, Portland is predominantly a 19th century city, built in the days of its greatest prosperity as a seaport and railroad center. After decades of decline following World War II, it has re-emerged as a dynamic postindustrial place: a center of finance, health and social services, tourism, and the arts. Yet, in spite of its modern commercialism and tourism, Portland remains a palpable historical place, and that is perhaps its great appeal. Its compact geography, preserved built environment, cultural amenities, and human scale have contributed to its late-twentieth-century resurgence. These features must be preserved as we move to the future.

When New York's magnificent Pennsylvania Station was demolished in 1963, it prompted renowned Yale architectural historian Vincent Scully to lament, "Once we entered the city like a god; one scuttles in now like a rat." The furor over the demolition of such a well-known landmark is often cited as a catalyst for the architectural preservation movement in the United States. So too in Portland, where the loss of Union Station and the old Post Office led to the formation of Greater Portland Landmarks to help protect the city's architectural heritage. .

For the first time, this book brings together vintage photographs of Portland and contemporary color images of the same scene side-by-side, providing a new awareness that, while much has been lost, much also remains. As you enjoy these photographs and rediscover Portland, perhaps for the first time, let us remind our selves that we must work together to find new ways to maintain the character, quality, and continuity of this beautiful City by the Sea.

John R. Moon
Falmouth, Maine
December 2010

Chapter One – Downtown and Bayside

Portland rests largely on a three-mile-long peninsula, shaped like a giant saddle with hills at both ends, and surrounded on three sides by the waters of Casco Bay and Back Cove. In the middle of the saddle, at the very heart of the city, lies Monument Square. This panoramic view of Portland shows the scene from the top floor of the city's first "skyscraper", the newly completed Fidelity Building of 1910, built in Monument Square where the former Deering Block once stood. At lower left is the Edwards and Walker hardware store (formerly the United States Hotel), while straight ahead is Middle Street, winding its way down to another famous landmark, the Falmouth Hotel, built in 1868 by John Bundy Brown. In the distance lies Portland Harbor and the islands of Casco Bay. The building on the horizon at right is most likely the Ottawa House on Cushing's Island, built in 1862 by Lemuel Cushing, who was hoping to attract a Canadian clientele there. Note the length of the breakwater at Bug Light, before it was shortened by filling in. (For a modern day equivalent of this scene, see Appendix A on page 175.)

The H.J. Libby House of 1852-53 on Congress Square Around 1925

At the northwest corner of Congress and High Streets once stood the Italianate double house of H.J. Libby. Built in 1852-53, this lovely home was designed by Charles A. Alexander (1827-1888) and was known for its elaborately painted wall decorations. It was demolished in 1928 to make way for the State Building. Notice in this photograph from the mid 1920s how the area is still predominantly residential, and not part of "downtown" as we think of it in the modern sense. In the center of the square an officer stands in a signal box to direct traffic, increasingly dominated by the automobile. (See also Appendix B on page 176.)

The State Building of 1929 was designed by Herbert W. Rhodes (1886-1956) and provides retail and office space. It is also home to the State Theater, the last of the pre-World War II cinemas left in downtown Portland. The Baxter Memorial Library of 1887-88 (shown at left on the opposite page but not visible here) is just to the left of the State Building, which now dominates the square at the corner of Congress and High Streets. The library was a gift to the city by James Phinney Baxter and served readers for nearly a century before becoming part of the Maine College of Art. It was designed by Francis H. Fassett (1823-1908).

The Rines Brothers Company Around 1912

This wonderful photograph dates from 1912, and shows the front of the Rines Brothers Company Store in the J.B. Brown Memorial Building on Congress Street. Everyone in the picture is wearing a hat. During this time, fashions held a great deal of embedded power, as indeed they still do today, and clothing expressed much about the wearer. Whether small specialty shops or large department stores, retail stores like this one lined the streets of Portland. At this time, Congress Street from Monument Square to Congress Square was becoming Portland's leading retail shopping district, with four major department stores.

In addition to the Rines Brothers Company Store, the other major department stores along this section of Congress Street were Eastman Brothers and Bancroft; Porteous, Mitchell, and Braun; and J.R. Libby, none of which are in business today. More than any other single factor, the popularity of and widespread use of the automobile is probably responsible for the eventual demise of the downtown shopping district, beginning in the 1960's and culminating in the 1970's. Maine's first shopping mall, the Maine Mall, opened in South Portland in 1969, and things have never been the same since. Today, art galleries occupy this site.

Trolleys on Congress Street Around 1928

Electric cars – or trolleys – brought real change to the lives of Portlanders. The Portland Railroad Company opened its original horsecar line, running 3.3 miles from Monument Square, downtown, to Morrill's Corner, Deering, on October 12, 1863. This line was electrified in 1891, and soon thereafter the company moved to electrify all lines. Electrification was a welcome innovation. This scene shows a busy day on Congress Street in the late 1920's in front of the Porteous, Mitchell, and Braun Company department store. The crowds have gathered to celebrate some special event, perhaps even the Lindbergh flight.

The same scene today shows much change. Electric trolleys no longer travel the streets of Portland, and the crowds of people downtown are noticeably thinner. The former Porteous, Mitchell, and Braun Company department store has closed for good, now home to the Maine College of Art. The left half of this beautiful building was built in 1904 by William Miller, who operated the Boston Shoe Store there until 1906, when he sold to Porteous, which added the right half in 1911. Designed by Penn Varney of Lynn, Massachusetts, the Renaissance Revival terra-cotta façade was carefully replicated in the expansion by George Burnham.

Shaw's Supermarket in the Deering Block Around 1900

This is a nice view of the Deering Block on Monument Square around 1900. The Nickel Theater operated here, as did Westerson's Stationery Store. Notice also the Shaw's Supermarket. Vermont native George C. Shaw moved to Portland in 1860 and opened a small shop downtown called Shaw's China Tea Store, employing as Asian man named Ah Foo as a tea expert. With success carrying tea and coffee, Shaw expanded to include fresh foods and groceries, and opened a second store at 580 Congress Street in 1872. By the turn-of-the-century, business was so good that he needed this additional store on Monument Square.

The Deering Block has long ago vanished, replaced in 1909-10 by Portland's very first "skyscraper", the ten-story Fidelity Building, designed by G. Henri Desmond of Boston. Both the Fidelity Building and the later Chapman Building of 1924 (today's "Time and Temperature" Building just across Preble Street) were planned to have a bank at street level. Comparing this photograph to the one on page 18, it is evident that the Fidelity Building sits on the same footprint as the old Deering Block, thus explaining its shape. In the 1990's, it was purchased by Elizabeth Noyce and now houses the Maine Bank & Trust Company.

Preble Street Around 1900

In this picture taken around the turn of the century, we are standing at the head of Preble Street and looking out over the waters of Back Cove. Just like today, people can be seen standing on the corner waiting for cars to pass, but the cars they waited for were not automobiles, but trolleys, like the Westbrook car shown here near the intersection. The Portland Railroad Company, operators of the trolleys, had a waiting room on the corner at right in the old Deering Block. Half way down the street on the right is the John J. Frye firm, makers of plows. On the left corner is the Preble House Hotel, once the site of the Preble Mansion, which then housed the T.F. Foss & Sons furniture store. Keith's Theater is farther down the street, and beyond that is the entrance to the Wadsworth Hotel.

In 1881, historian Edward Elwell wrote eloquently about the lovely views to be seen of the surrounding countryside from the very heart of the city at Monument Square: "We know of no city where, from the very center of its business streets, one may look out upon such beautiful views of land and water as may be seen from the heart of our city. Stand, at the hour of sunset, at the head of Preble Street, and look out over the waters of the Cove, reflecting the hues of the sunset sky; upon the green fields and tree-crowned summits of Deering, and tell us if anything can be finer." Today, the Fidelity Building of 1910 replaces the Deering Block on the right, while the Chapman Building of 1924 replaces the Preble Hotel on the left. The street was named in honor of Commodore Edward Preble.

The Y.M.C.A. Building of 1897, later known as The Libby Building, now the Portland Museum of Art

In this view of Congress Square taken around the turn-of-the-century, we can see what was then the new Y.M.C.A building of 1897, designed by Frederick A. Tompson, on the site of the former Matthew Cobb Mansion that was built in 1801 (see Appendix R on page 192 for more on the Cobb Mansion). After 1927, when the present Y.M.C.A. was built on Forest Avenue, it became known as the Libby Building, and served a variety of functions though the 1970's. Since 1983 it has been the site of the Payson Wing of the Portland Museum of Art. At left is the H.H. Hay and Sons Block designed by Charles Q. Clapp in 1826.

The Payson Wing of the Portland Museum of Art was designed by Henry Cobb, a descendant of Matthew Cobb, who once lived on this corner. The billboard-like front recalls the Doges Palace in Venice, while the use of arched motifs echoes the work of Sir John Soane. To the left of the art museum is the present day Children's Museum of Maine, with its long history of adaptive reuse. Built as the Portland Theater in 1830, it was the Free Street Baptist Church from 1836 to 1926, when it was acquired by the Portland Chamber of Commerce. The Chamber hired the Stevens firm to remodel the building to the appearance it has today.

"New" High Street as it looked around 1900

After the Great Fire of 1866, residential construction spread westward. The area between Deering, Mellen, and High Streets and Park Avenue was once known as Deering Pasture. The neighborhood was developed with substantial homes like those shown here on the east side of New High Street, as the section from Congress Square to Park Avenue was once known. This view is standing on the corner of Cumberland Avenue looking up High Street toward Congress Square. An example of the fine residences being built on Deering Street at this time can be seen in the home of Thomas Brackett Reed in Appendix N on page 188.

Beautiful homes no longer line this section of High Street, which has been taken over by the Eastland Hotel and a new parking garage. Edward Elwell wrote of this area in 1881: "We went there at sunset to sit on the ledges and watch the sun go down behind the hills, shedding a last lingering glory on the clouds, which the tranquil waters of the Cove gave back with answering colors. Wealth and taste have here been lavished in the construction of some of these modern residences, and the street, though still new, and bordering on vacant spaces, is one of the handsomest in the city, representing the wealth and taste of today."

The New Eastland Hotel, June 15, 1927

This remarkable photograph of the Eastland Hotel taken from Deering Street shows the hotel shortly after its opening in 1927. Charles Lindbergh had just made his historic solo flight across the Atlantic Ocean, and in Portland Henry Rines had just created one of the most beautiful hotels in America. Billed by the local press as "the Forest City's supreme symbol of elegance," the hotel opened its doors on June 15, 1927. The $2 million, 12-story Eastland Hotel was heralded as "the most important building project that has ever been carried out in this city." The hotel was designed by local architect Herbert Rhodes and featured a brick, limestone and plaster exterior with steel casement windows. Henry P. Rines and his wife Adeline (the first woman to practice law in Cumberland County) were frequent travelers to Europe and the Middle East. Their travels impressed them and the lobby and restaurants of their new hotel were fashioned after their favorite locations abroad. The hotel entrance was designed to resemble an old Spanish patio with stone benches, a colorful red and yellow striped awning, slate floor, and red tiled roofs for balcony effects. The steps beside the front door led downstairs to the grill, (then called the Sunrise Gateway Room) and a barbershop. This room was later renovated to become the popular post-war Polynesian lounge, the Hawaiian Hut and in 1990 became the Sonesta's state-of-the-art function room, Cumberland Hall (now known as the Eastland Park Hotel's Longfellow Hall).

Here is a nice picture of the hotel as it stands today, as beautiful as ever. Henry Rines spared no expense when it came to interior appointments for his new hotel. The lobby featured a beamed ceiling supported by massive pillars. The wrought iron candelabras were copied from the old fixtures in a Madrid café . Several wall sconces in the lobby cleverly simulated old Spanish flowerpots with trailing vines. The street level shopping arcade included a beauty shop, "Ask Mr. Foster" travel newsstand, and the House of Conant Tailor and Valet Service. A Delicatessen was later established to provide bakery products and coffee to the hotel apartment tenants. The Danish Tea Room (now the Greenhouse, a private function room) was an authentic reproduction of an 18th century tavern which was located in the marketplace of Ribe, the capitol of medieval Denmark. The tavern had not been remodeled in over 150 years, and the Rines family used it as the model for their new restaurant. Old pieces of Baroque-style furniture were imported from Denmark to furnish "The Skenkstuen" (the room where patrons are served). These pieces included pine tables worn smooth by years of use, corner cupboards, an antique clock and a billegerovn heating chamber that drew hot air from the chimney in the adjacent room. The Spanish Baronial dining room, later named the State of Maine Ballroom, featured an oak floor, carved adornments on the entranceway and balcony, and antique Spanish lanterns. The beam supports were decorated with sculpted armor. Charles Lindbergh himself visited the Eastland in July 1927. "The Lone Eagle" flew into Old Orchard Beach, spoke to crowds at Deering Oaks Park, returned to the Eastland to rest and was honored at a banquet attended by 700 people in this room (now called the Eastland Ballroom).

Lower Hays Drug Store

It was hatmaker Byron Greenough who built the three-story brick block on the triangular lot at the corner of Free and Middle Streets in 1848. His hat and fur business was replaced in 1856 by H.H. Hay's drugstore. Ever since then, Portlanders have come to associate this location as the home of "lower" Hay's drugstore. Later, in 1912, Hay's would open a second store at the other end of Free Street, known as the "uptown" store. The lower store barely escaped the Great Fire of 1866 and operated at this location until 1964. A fourth floor designed by John Calvin Stevens was added to this Lower Hay Block in 1919.

One of the great things about the city of Portland is that you can still walk about town and see many of these wonderful 19th century buildings one hundred to one hundred and fifty years after they were built. This is the Lower Hay Block as it appears today. The little vestibule on the end (at left) has been done away with, and the entrances have changed, but the building itself it still very much there, adapted for a new use in a new age. At one time, Middle Street used to wind up from the Old Port district and meet with Congress Street at Monument Square. Now this entire block has been "pedestrianized", and the street no longer exists.

This is Congress Street as it looked from a City Hall window around 1920. At the right is the Davis Block, housing Gray's Portland Business College, attorney's offices, the Frank C. White shoe store, and R. Cutler Libby insurance agency. Erected in 1855, the building was demolished in 1947 to make way for the Gannett Building. Across Market Street, where Central Fire Station now stands, is a building housing Chemical Engine No. 1, the City Liquor Agency, Steam Fire Engine No. 5, Ladder No. 1, and the fire chief's office. Beyond is the F.F. Foss & Sons furniture manufacturing plant, the R.J. Libby Laundry, and the Ward 3 wardrooms overlooking the Congress and Pearl Street intersection. At the head of Myrtle Street is the Heseltine & Tuttle Co. drug store and the New York Cleansing, Pressing and Repairing Company. (For more on the history of this, the City of Portland's fourth City Hall, see Appendix C on page 177.)

Portland's first city hall was the old Market House on Monument Square, built in 1825, but later turned into a city hall in 1832 when it was modified by Charles Quincy Clapp. One of the things he did was remove the original tower, which found a home across town in 1834 when it was placed atop Westbrook Junior College's brand new Alumni Hall (see Appendix Q, page 191 for more about the old City Hall cupola). This site, at the head of Myrtle Street, was home to Portland's second city hall, built in 1858-64, but destroyed in the Great Fire of 1866. A third city hall was built on the same site, like a Phoenix rising from the ashes, but it too burned on January 24, 1908. The present city hall of 1912 is the city's fourth, and the third to be built on this site. The new fire station across the street, built in 1923, was designed by William R. Miller and Raymond J. Mayo in the Beaux-Arts style to complement nearby government buildings.

A View of Longfellow Square in the 1920s

This charming 1920's view of Longfellow Square is looking south down the original section of State Street from Congress Street toward York Street. Clearly seen in this particular view are the double rows of elm trees planted in 1800, and arching to meet above the center of the street, forming a natural canopy to provide shade on a hot summer day. On the left, the Dr. Israel T. Dana house of 1878, by Francis H. Fassett, had been converted to commercial use by the time this photograph was taken. When Longfellow died in 1882, Portland honored its most famous son by naming the square for him

There used to be a rotary here that automobiles could drive around, but as with other sections of town the street has been filled in with sidewalk to make it more pedestrian friendly. Another change is that State Street no longer accommodates two-way traffic. It is now a one-way street that comes up the hill from Deering Oaks to Longfellow Square, then continues one-way down State Street to the bridge. Since 1888, the bronze figure of the seated poet by Franklin Simmons has gazed down Congress Street from atop a granite pedestal designed by Francis H. Fassett. Sadly, the beautiful elm trees have all now been lost to disease.

The Preble Mansion as it looked around 1860

This is an early photograph from about 1860 of the Commodore Edward Preble Mansion, designed in 1805 by Alexander Parris (1780-1852). In 1801, Preble (1761-1807) had married Mary Deering (1770-1851), the wealthy daughter of Kittery boat-builder Nathaniel Deering (1739-1795), and then went on to earn fame as the hero of the 1801-1805 war against the Barbary pirates of North Africa under his flagship the *U.S.S. Constitution*. Ill from either tuberculosis or stomach cancer, Preble retired from the Navy in 1805, returned to his native Portland, and commissioned Parris to build this new home later that year. Construction began in 1806, just as Mary gave birth to their only son, Edward Deering Preble (1806-1846). Sadly, the commodore died at his Middle Street home in August 1807 before the mansion was completed, and he himself never lived there. His wife Mary finished the job, however, and moved into the new home in 1808, where she lived until her own death in 1851. Shortly after this photograph was taken, the home was enlarged on both sides and became the Preble House Hotel, one of the finest hotels in the city until it was demolished in 1924 to make way for the Chapman Building, today's Time and Temperature Building.

Today's "Time and Temperature" Building started out life in 1924 as the Chapman Building, and before that it was the site of the Preble House hotel. This was Portland's second skyscraper, coming some years after the Fidelity Building of 1910 just across Preble Street. The twelve-story Chapman Building contained forty stores, many offices, and the Chapman National Bank. It's most unusual feature, however, was an arcade that ran from Congress Street to the Preble Street entrance of Keith's Theater (later known as the Civic Theater). The walkway was lined with shops and can be viewed as a precursor to today's malls.

The Asa Clapp Mansion at Congress and Elm Around 1920

Historian William David Barry writes eloquently of Asa Clapp: "By 1800 transatlantic shipping was booming as never before in the rough-edged, rough-and-ready city of Portland. The wharves and bulwarks of the country's sixth largest port creaked and groaned under the lashings of hemp warp and the rumbling of heavy cargoes. It was here in this rugged, sea-scoured town of shore huggers and blue-water men that the merchant Asa Clapp amassed one of the republic's first great fortunes, enjoying the comfort of a palatial mansion at a time when most Americans lived close to the soil." This was the home he built for himself at the corner of Elm and Congress Streets. (For another view of this beautiful home, including more on the life of Asa Clapp, see Appendix O on page 189.)

Once a penniless farm boy, later a swashbuckling captain, Asa Clapp (1762-1848) was portrayed in the early 1800's as an American aristocrat. For signals of his incoming ships, bearing cargoes of Cuban molasses, German glassware, or even Russian featherbeds, Portland's leading merchant prince turned his eyes to the signal flags flying from the Observatory atop Munjoy Hill, built in 1807 by Lemuel Moody. All he had to do was walk up to the octagonal cupola on his roof and look up the hill to see them. By 1924, the desirable Congress Street location of the Clapp Mansion had become quite valuable, and the once proud residence of one of Portland's favorite sons was torn down and replaced by this seven-story commercial block, directly across Elm Street from the Portland Public Library.

Forest Avenue Around 1920

This is a very interesting photograph of Forest Avenue around 1920. We are standing at the intersection of Forest Avenue and Park Avenue looking north on Forest Avenue in the direction of Woodfords. On the right is the site of today's Portland Post Office, which was built in 1933-34 to designs by the Stevens firm. This shows what was there before the post office: homes and a few businesses perhaps. On the left is a not very pretty looking Deering Oaks. The eight acre section between State Street and Forest Avenue was acquired between 1893 and 1923. In the left distance is the Huston Baking Company.

Thanks to some more trees and lots of landscaping, things look considerably more inviting in this view of Forest Avenue than the 1920 view. Steps to the new Portland Post Office of 1933-34 can be seen right, though the building itself is just out of view. The Huston Baking Company shown in the earlier photograph, further along down Forest Avenue, was known as the "Baker of Better Biscuits since 1869". Their new bakery was built in 1919-20 to designs by Webster and Libby. It was later used by the National Biscuit Company and, in 1993, it was remodeled to become one of the libraries of the University of Southern Maine.

Portland High School in the 1920s

Here is a great photograph of Portland High School taken shortly after the newly remodeled and enlarged school was opened on February 15, 1919. Planning for the new school had begun in 1912 because the original 1863 school was no longer adequate; by 1915, a school which had been built for 650 students had a registration of 1209. Only 800 of these were actually in the school itself. 275 were accommodated in City Hall, while another 120 were housed in Gray's Business College. In addition, manual training and domestic science were taught in the Walker Building. Using four buildings to house one high school was a situation which could not be allowed to continue for long. The cause of the growth of the student population was twofold. Portland was undergoing a period of rapid growth, sparked by an influx of immigrants. Between 1890 and 1920 the population of the city nearly doubled. In addition, the attitude of the public toward high school was changing; it was no longer considered exclusively for those going on to college. Enrollment at PHS thus tripled between 1900 and 1918.

After hearing such suggestions as Forest Avenue, Deering Oaks, and Lincoln Park, the building committee decided to add on to the old building. With the 1863 school forming the center wing, the new E-shaped Portland High School was designed to take in nearly all the property between Elm and Chestnut Streets. Henry Desmond of Boston and Miller and Mayo of Portland were selected as the architects. In 1916, while classes went on in the old building, construction was begun around it. The fence seen in the picture on page 187 was removed from the front of the school and placed on the Congress Street side of Eastern Cemetery where it still stands. Original plans called for the new school to open in the fall of 1917, but a shortage of materials caused by World War I held up construction. Finally, on February 15, 1919, the building was officially opened. Principal William B. Jack stressed that the new school would truly be the citizen's school, "an American school and like America its doors are open to anyone who knocks." (See also Appendix D, page 178 for more on the history of Portland High School.)

Chestnut Street Methodist Church

The Chestnut Street Methodist Church is a graceful example of brick and brownstone Gothic Revival architecture. As originally built in 1856-57 from designs by Charles A. Alexander, the church featured a pair of minaret-like spires, which were removed, leaving the two octagonal towers to frame the central entrance and the large arched window above it. The 152-year old church is one of those architectural masters that stir up strong reactions. It was designed to awe its occupants and reinforce their faith: soaring wooden arches leap down its long sanctuary to an ornate, white altar meant to be a replica of the church façade, but rather resembling a giant wedding cake. The organ case dates from 1836. Light seeps into the church through a series of stained-glass windows shaped like spears, possibly by C.H. Farley, and a massive Rose window, believed to have come from Florence in the mid-1800s glows above the church's main doorway. The front façade is adorned with two windows shaped as trefoils, an ancient symbol made of three overlapping almond-like shapes that symbolize unity. The trefoil is a common design in Gothic architecture. Originally built in 1812, the Chestnut Street Church is considered to be the Mother Church of Portland Methodism. The elegant patent-pressed brick, flanked by two slender spires, exhibits a distinctive balance in the city. The steeply sloping roof, buttressed by three pointed arch doorways, open timbering and hand-crafted woodwork, are all characteristic of the Gothic style.

The beautiful Chestnut Street Methodist Church, shown here from Portland High School's Freshman Alley (the only vantage point from which you can now capture this much of a view of the church in today's congested downtown neighborhood) was purchased in 2007 by Peter and Anne Verrill, successful owners of the Foreside Tavern in Falmouth, for $675,000 after its Methodist congregation had abandoned it two years earlier. It has now been transformed into a new restaurant called Grace. The building had no working electricity, gas or water; its brownstone façade was badly weathered; and the walls had gaping holes exposing brick. To help pay for the $2 million restoration, the couple applied for state and federal historic tax credits, which were designed to make the preservation of antique buildings, like this one, financially feasible and competitive with new construction. Spending $150 per square foot, the Verrills converted the 5,000 square foot first floor into a kitchen and dining room, with a capacity for at least 100 diners. A free-standing bar was built next to an open kitchen set in front of the semi-circular apse. Cleverly, the bar is shaped like the church's trefoil windows, carved to look like stylized three-petal flowers. These windows – two are set on either side of the church's rose window – have also become Grace's logo. The balcony, which wraps around the nave on three sides, holds more tables and another bar and lounge area. Perhaps most special of all are the two tall brick towers that were once topped with wooden spires that reached 110 feet, but were dismantled for safety reasons more than 50 years ago. The Verrills are now using these circular towers as wine cellars, with semi-circular racks of wine affixed to the walls. Built inside the foot of each tower is a separate men's and ladies room, an innovative idea and very quaint.

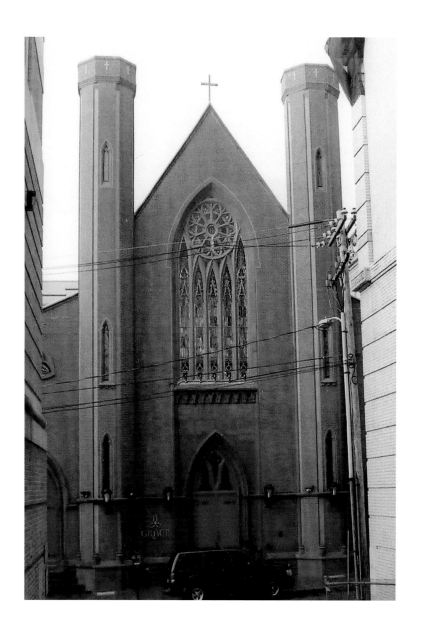

It is fitting to end this chapter where it began, at Portland's Monument Square. On the left is an early view of what was then known as Market Square. The columned building was originally constructed as Portland's Market House in 1825 to provide stalls for selling produce on the ground floor, with a hall for militia training above. It was designed by John Kimball Jr. (1783-1865). In 1832, it was modified into a Greek Revival style building by Charles Q. Clapp (1799-1868) and became Portland's first City Hall. The domed building in the distance is the city's third city hall, replacing the second one that burned in the great fire. The photograph on the right shows Monument Square today, quite changed from the way it looked a century ago.

Chapter Two – Munjoy Hill and the East End

The year is 1928, and three children pause to look at a dog in front of E.P. Quinn's Coal and Wood store located at 43 Washington Avenue, at the foot of Munjoy Hill, the moment captured on film. The building, directly adjacent to the former J.J. Nissen Baking Company on Washington Avenue, has since been torn down. Its replacement is now home to a busy Coffee By Design store frequented by hill residents, and others. The Munjoy Hill section of Portland has always been a special place, physically set off from the rest of the peninsula, and to this day boasting a very strong sense of community. Howard Reiche, Jr. said it best, perhaps, recalling his youth growing up on the hill during the 1930's: "Munjoy Hill, a whole bunch of people who lived and fit together quite smoothly."

A Drawing of Munjoy Hill as it looked in the 1840s by Charles Goodhue

Charles Quincy Goodhue (1835-1910) was a marble cutter at Enoch Thompson's Monument Works located at Preble Street and Cumberland Avenue, as well as a volunteer fireman. During the last twenty years of his life, he made a remarkable series of drawings to set down a visual memoir of the Portland of his youth – a city that had disappeared in the flames of the Great Fire. The shape of early 19th century Portland would be available only through written descriptions and a scattering of paintings and daguerreotypes were it not for his drawings. This one shows Munjoy Hill as it looked in the 1840's, still largely open pasture used for grazing cows. In early deeds, land was sold with consideration listed as so many "Cow Rights," one being equal to about three acres of land.

This photograph, taken from the third floor of the old North School, captures roughly the same scene as portrayed by Goodhue. Congress Street rises up from the left to the summit of Munjoy Hill, 161 feet above sea level, and Mountfort Street runs to the right in the foreground on its way down to Fore Street and the ancient harbor, very near to where George Cleeve first settled the area in 1632. Eastern Cemetery, shown, dates back to the 17th century and is Portland's oldest burying ground. In 1858, the city suspended most burials there. Above the churches, businesses, apartments and homes, the timeless 82 foot Observatory still looms proudly at the top of the hill. To residents and visitors alike, it has become a symbol, not only of the neighborhood, but of Portland itself.

Morning Street and the Munjoy Hill Loop

Most of us have childhood memories of big snowstorms that left huge piles of snow, and maybe that's because we were all so much smaller then. But seeing is believing! This is Morning Street on Munjoy Hill, and these snow banks are the real thing. A child playing on the sidewalk could not see the street. Morning Street was part of the Munjoy Hill "loop" of the trolley system. As Howard Reiche, Jr. recalls, "it was great fun as a child to build forts and tunnels with popup holes in these long, high snow banks. You could pop up and pelt the trolley cars with snowballs and duck down before they could figure out who did it."

Because of the Munjoy Hill "loop" of the trolley system, there was no end of the line. The trolley came up Congress Street, turned right onto Morning Street, onto the Eastern Promenade by Fort Allen Park, right onto Atlantic and back to Congress Street and downtown. Again, according to Howard Reiche, Jr., "When the trolley came up over the hill and stopped at Feldman's Drugstore, you could quietly lower the rear cowcatcher without attracting any attention. Then you could hook a ride around the loop and jump off by Feldman's Drugstore where you started." Here, the trolley tracks are still visible beneath today's pavement.

The Portland Company Around 1900

The Portland Company on the waterfront at the foot of Munjoy Hill has roots going back to the 1840s. Established in 1847 by John Alfred Poor, whose enthusiasm for railroads included building his own locomotives, it developed a national reputation for constructing locomotives, boilers, and other machinery. Housed in a huge complex of brick buildings on Fore Street, the company also manufactured shell casings and boats during wartime; it eventually diversified into automobiles, steam boilers, and anything else that would turn a profit. (See also Appendix P on page 190 for more on the life of John Alfred Poor.)

It is great fun today to wander around at the foot of Fore Street and see the many remaining brick buildings, like this one, that constitute the Portland Company complex. The area is now home to a variety of businesses, from yacht services to sailing lessons. The Maine Narrow Gauge Railroad maintains its offices and a museum there, where visitors can not only see exhibits from the great railroad era of a previous century, but also take a ride on a real train, which travels along the shore at the base of the Eastern Promenade. Various special programs are run throughout the year, including the annual Flower Show each year in Spring.

Longfellow's Birthplace, Corner of Fore and Hancock Streets, Around 1890

The poet Henry Wadsworth Longfellow (1807-1882) was born in this home at the corner of Hancock and Fore Streets. Hancock Street (at left) was laid out in 1800. That year William Campbell bought a lot from the Rev. Elijah Kellogg, Sr. and built the three story home. Captain Samuel Stephenson purchased the home in 1804. In 1807, the year Longfellow was born, his parents were spending the winter there with his father's sister, who was married to Stephenson, away at the time in the West Indies on business. Stephenson lost the house during the Embargo of 1807 and moved to Gorham early the next year.

When the house was in its prime, it stood a little back from the shore and from its windows was an unobstructed view of the harbor. Reflecting the widespread enthusiasm for Longfellow's poetry, the International Longfellow Society acquired the property in 1914 and operated it as a literary shrine. Tastes in poetry changed, later efforts to preserve the house failed, and it was torn down in 1955. Since then the place where the structure stood has been under tons of iron in the yard of a Portland Foundry. In 2009, this Residence Inn was built there. Mounted on a small boulder in front of the Inn is a plaque marking the site today.

Faded and worn, this is a remarkable early photograph of the Portland Observatory atop Munjoy Hill, dating from the 1880s. As Edward Elwell wrote in 1881: "At the Observatory we strike the old sod again. This red-shingled tower is 82 feet high, and was built in 1807 for the purpose of signalizing shipping approaching the harbor. Since its erection, many an eye has been gladdened by the flag thrown out on one of its three flagstaffs, indicating the approach of some long-absent ship; and many a storm-tossed vessel has been saved from wreck by the succor sent out through timely intelligence from the watch-tower, where the sailor's good genius sits up aloft and sweeps the horizon with his glass." Note the home to the right of the Observatory, and the one in the left foreground.

After the demolition of Portland's Union Station in 1961, Greater Portland Landmarks was formed to take up the banner of historic preservation in the city of Portland. Fittingly, its logo depicts the Portland Observatory. In 1807 Captain Lemuel Moody promoted the building of the Observatory on the highest point on Munjoy Hill. It was a vital communication center for the seafaring town. Ships in distress could be spotted by its telescope; each shipowner had a specially colored flag flown from the tower to alert the owner that his ship was nearing port. Wives of Portland seamen watched the tower to see when their loved ones were coming home. The Observatory today remains one of Portland's most popular tourist attractions, and the homes at right and in the foreground still exist.

Charles Codman, *The Entertainment of the Boston Rifle Rangers at the Portland Observatory*, 1830

Charles Codman (1800-1842) was a noted landscape painter whose work was "discovered" in 1828 by contemporary art critic John Neal (1793-1876). Probably from Boston, he was apprenticed to the ornamental painter John Ritto Pennimans, and began as a decorative painter but eventually produced mature works of romance and beauty. After moving to Portland in 1822, he designed and painted five fireboards for the Portland mansion of shipbuilder James Deering. One of these fireboards, *View of Diamond Cove from Great Diamond Island, 1829*, was reproduced in print form, along with *The Entertainment of the Boston Rifle Rangers at the Portland Observatory, 1830*, helping to spread Codman's fame. The latter painting, shown here, depicts how Munjoy Hill looked in 1830.

After almost two centuries of residential and commercial development on the hill, it is difficult to try to photograph Munjoy Hill as it looked in Codman's day. The sheer number of houses built on the hill since then make it next to impossible to stand on the ground and view the Observatory from the same vantage point as Codman saw it. Perseverance and imagination pay off, however. There is only one possible place in the entire city where a similar view could be obtained, and that is at the top of the old Shailer School on North Street. From a balcony there, we look out over the rooftops of surrounding homes to the Observatory on the left and the entrance to Portland harbor in the distance. Cows no longer graze on the hill, and land is no longer listed in deeds as so many "Cow Rights".

The Grand Army of the Republic Marching Down Congress Street, 1885

The Grand Army of the Republic was an organization of Civil War veterans who held an encampment and parade in Portland in 1885, celebrating the 20th anniversary of the ending of the Civil War. This was the scene that day as the procession marched down Congress Street from the summit of Munjoy Hill on its way to Market Square. To capture the moment, someone leaned out the window and snapped this picture. At the top of the hill, standing like a sentinel as it always has since the day it was built in 1807, is Lemuel Moody's signal tower, now known as the Portland Observatory, and next to it, the Methodist Church.

Just like the photographer from 1885, the author leaned out a third floor window of this building to get the same vantage point for this photograph. Lemuel Moody's maritime signal tower still stands, of course, a gift to the city from Moody's descendants in 1939. Many of the homes along Congress Street, however, appear to have been either replaced or modified, as they simply do not match up on a one-to-one basis. The Observatory used a system of flags to tell ship owners when a ship had been spotted in the harbor so all could be readied for its arrival. The flags still fly at this last remaining signal tower in the country.

July 4, 1898 on the Eastern Promenade

Earlier, on page 58, we saw the Grand Army of the Republic celebrating the 20th anniversary of the ending of the Civil War with an encampment on the Eastern Promenade and a parade down Congress Street to Monument Square. This is typical of countless events, celebrations and get-togethers that Portlanders have been participating in on Munjoy Hill ever since the city was founded. One event that gets repeated every year is the annual celebration of the Fourth of July Holiday. Portland residents traditionally celebrate the 4th with a fireworks display on the Eastern Promenade. The date for this one was July 4, 1898.

Over 110 years later, the foot of Congress Street is still the gateway to the Eastern Promenade, which remains the most significant land feature of Munjoy Hill. Laid out by the city in 1837, the Eastern Promenade was designed by the Olmstead Brothers with amazing water vistas wrapping from the sunset view at the Loring Memorial above the shore for over a mile to a sunrise view over the Calendar Islands of Casco Bay and Portland Head Light, and ending at Fort Allen Park with a full sweep of Portland Harbor. And let's not forget East End Beach, a favorite of kayakers, families, and, after 5 PM, dog owners and their pets!

Portland Company Cars on the Eastern Promenade

In this 1909 picture, eleven new Knox automobiles are lined up along the Eastern Promenade for a Portland Company publicity photograph. All of these automobiles have just been sold, as all have 1909 Maine license plates with consecutive numbers hanging from their front axles. At the time this photograph was taken the Portland Company was the sole distributor of Knox automobiles and trucks in the state of Maine, and it often used the Eastern Promenade locale as a scenic setting to showcase their automobiles. The two homes on the right are at the very end of Morning Street as it comes down to meet the promenade.

As can be seen in this contemporary photograph, little has changed in this Eastern Promenade neighborhood over the past one hundred years. The two homes on the right are still standing at the foot of Morning Street, and the view here of Portland Harbor is as striking as ever. Both the Western and Eastern Promenades were first laid out by the city in 1837. Surprisingly, not everyone was in favor of the plan. An 1836 *Eastern Argus* article noted: "They may be very pleasant for those that keep horses and gig and have nothing else to do but ride about, but they will not be the least advantage to nine-tenths of the taxpayers of the city."

Grand Trunk Station from the Rear

This is a stunning and rare view of the Grand Trunk terminal as passengers would have seen it upon arrival on a train (or departure, too, for that matter). The tracks veering off to the left are headed on to Commercial Street where they eventually met up with the Boston and Maine and Maine Central Railroads at Union Station on the other side of town. The Grand Trunk terminal was built in 1903 for the Grand Trunk Railway, which had connected Montreal with Portland since 1853. The imposing station and railroad office building were designed by the Detroit firm of Spier and Rohr. Only the office building on the left remains today.

It is sad in a way to see what has happened to this section of Portland, but progress marches on. The view that once greeted passengers of the Grand Trunk Railway upon arrival in Portland is now greatly changed. In fact, if it were not for the remaining Grand Trunk office building shown here on the left, one would barely be able to recognize this scene at all. The proud Grand Trunk terminal building was demolished in 1966, a few years after rail passenger service ended, and the mighty grain elevators which once stood on this spot were demolished shortly thereafter, making room for the parking lot we see on the site today.

Two Women in a Car on the Eastern Promenade

Two women are enjoying a brisk morning ride along the Eastern Promenade in their spiffy new 1910 Cole automobile, sold then by the Portland Company at their adjoining facility just below the promenade on Fore Street. Pictured are Martha Reynolds at the wheel, wife of George F. Reynolds, the works manager of the Portland Company, and her passenger Ellen H. Russell, wife of Harry H. Russell, president of E.T. Burrowes Company. With no top on the car and very little heat to warm them up, the women are dressed suitably for the occasion. With a hand cranked starter, one wonders who helped them start the car this day.

One hundred years later, here we are at the same location along the Eastern Promenade, but with slightly less snow on the ground. The cars are no longer started with a hand crank, but motorists still come to this section of the city to enjoy the breathtaking views of Casco Bay. From all over the hill, residents come here not only in cars, but to walk, jog, ride a bicycle, sit on a park bench, or simply lay in the grass on a sunny day, taking advantage of ocean breezes that blow off the water in this picturesque part of the city. For countless Portlanders, the promenade remains as pleasant today as it must have been a century ago.

Portland Company Car on Eastern Promenade

These two men have to be either out of their minds or very brave souls, judging from the amount of snow on the ground. This is another photograph from the Portland Company Collection at the Maine Historical Society showing two men enjoying a winter time excursion on the Eastern Promenade in a brand new 1907 Knox runabout. Pictured are race car driver A.L. Dennison with passenger E.H. Cushman of the Portland Company. The Eastern Promenade locale is adjacent to the company's facilities at the foot of Fore Street and was used often as a place to display their new automobile lineup, apparently without regard to weather.

If you examine this photograph taken one hundred years later, the same house still stands in the background, although you will likely find no horses in the barn to the rear of the building. The move from horse-drawn transportation to automobiles had already begun when the earlier photograph was taken back in 1907. True, one had to be wealthy to afford these early automobiles; the technology was still in its infancy, and early cars were quite expensive for most people to own. Therefore, not many were able to afford them. But as the years passed, prices came down, thanks to Henry Ford, and the automobile was here to stay.

North School Around 1900

Let us return to Edward Elwell for a description of the North School in one of his celebrated walks about town: "At the corner of Congress and India Streets, where formerly the Thomas mansion stood, now rises the tall spire of the Second Universalist Church. Adjoining this church, on the east, stands the North School House, on the spot where, in the old grammar school, Master Whitmore flogged the boys for many a year. It is a huge, four-storied structure, of brick, containing a congeries of primary and grammar schools, comprising twenty-six teachers and twelve hundred scholars, all under one principal."

The photograph on the facing page shows the North grammar and primary school on Congress Street around 1900. It was built immediately after the Great Fire of 1866, and opened in 1867. This four story brick structure has a commanding view of the harbor and of Portland's oldest burying ground, Eastern Cemetery. It sits at the base of Munjoy Hill near the head of India Street in one of the oldest and most historically significant sections of Portland. Today, a new wing has been added and the building now serves as a subsidized home for the elderly. Many windows have been replaced improperly, but at least the clock still works!

St. Paul's Anglican Church

St. Paul's Anglican Church on the corner of Congress and Locust Streets is an exquisite example of Gothic Revival architecture that began to develop in Portland in the late 1840s. St. Paul's Parish was established in 1763, and services were held on Richmond Island in Casco Bay. The first building of the Parish at India and Fore Streets was burned by the British during the Revolutionary War; the second building was lost in the Great Fire of 1866. The present church, the third, dates to 1868 and was designed by George Brown Pelham (1831-1889), architect of the New York City Parks Department. The distinctive stained glass windows on the west wall symbolize the Holy Trinity; the Rose window over the altar contains the symbols of the first evangelists, Matthew, Mark, Luke and John.

Of special interest here is the later Gothic cottage, similar in exterior detail to Henry Rowe's John J. Brown House of 1845 (see Appendix E on page 179). Designed by George Pelham to adjoin the new St. Paul's Church, the rectory went up in 1869. The second St. Paul's structure, built in 1802 on Church Lane between Middle and Federal Streets, had been a solid brick, late eighteenth century design with a projecting central bell tower. When it burned in 1866, the new structures were appropriately and fashionably Gothic. The siding on the rectory, once covered over, has been restored to its original wood, cut and beveled to imitate stone, as in the Brown House. The delicately-pointed arcade, supported on slender colonettes and suggesting a cloister, is unique in present-day Portland.

St. Lawrence Church

The St. Lawrence Church on the corner of Congress and Munjoy Streets was, until recently, one of the city's most distinctive and dramatic examples of Queen Anne style. Erected by Congregationalists in 1897 from designs by Arthur Bates Jennings (1849-1927) of New York, the stone and slate-over-frame building was defined by its picturesque roofline and circular tower. The façade was distinguished by identical street-facing walls of arched windows and doorways. Decoration featured a large circular Rose window flanked by miniature attached turrets. The circular tower rose two stories and was capped by an open belfry.

After the church closed in 1985, a dwindling congregation of a few dozen dissolved and deconsecrated the building, and sold St. Lawrence Church in 1986. After several failed attempts to create a use for St. Lawrence, including creating a cultural center with Japanese partners, and after several changes of ownership, the parish house next door has become a popular performing arts center, known since January 2000 as the St. Lawrence Arts and Community Center. Efforts to save the dangerously unstable and crumbling church have failed, however, and the magnificent Portland landmark on Munjoy Hill was recently demolished

This drawing, sketched by Charles Goodhue around 1900, is all we have to visualize the Abyssinian Church as it once appeared at its home on Newbury Street in Portland. Unlike the Irish and the French Canadians, who came to Maine in the 19th century in waves, blacks settled individually from the earliest days. During the Federal Period black stevedores virtually controlled the longshore work at Portland (see, e.g., page 132), and the area around Hancock, Newbury and the Hill (above Mountfort) became a distinctly black neighborhood. The center of the Portland black community was the Abyssinian Church at the corner of Mountfort and Newbury Streets. According to Willis, the society was incorporated in 1828, and was later joined by 22 black members of the Second Parish Church. The Rev. Amos N. Freeman is mentioned as the earliest pastor. Its successor was Green Memorial A.M.E. Zion Church on Sheridan Street.

The Abyssinian Meeting House was constructed by free blacks in 1828 and became the cultural center of the community. Meetings, church services, concerts, a segregated public school, dinners and entertainment made the Abyssinian the center of political and social life which united the community throughout the 19th century. It closed in 1917 and was remodeled in 1924 as tenement apartments. Eventually, the city seized the building for unpaid taxes, and it sat vacant and deteriorating until 1998 when community leaders acquired it and founded the Committee to Restore the Abyssinian. It is presently engaged in a multi-year restoration effort, seen here in progress, to renovate the Abyssinian as a meeting place to celebrate the cultural heritage of African Americans in Maine. Now listed on the National Register of Historic Places and safe from demolition, this pivotal restoration project is poised to be of local, state and national significance.

An Aerial View of the Grand Trunk Station in 1963

This 1963 aerial view of Portland's East End is full of history, and shows the most ancient part of the city, going all the way back to its settlement in 1632 by George Cleeve and Richard Tucker, when it was known as Cleeve's or Falmouth Neck (the Native Americans knew this area as Machegonne). The name Casco Bay in fact derives from another Indian word: Aucocisco, meaning heron, a bird that once frequented these waters, as it still does today. (The next time you take a Casco Bay ferry, notice the names on the boats.) Cleeve and Tucker settled near the corner of the present day Fore and Hancock Streets, next to a "runnett" of water, which would put them right about in the center of the Grand Trunk Railway Terminal complex shown at lower left. This terminal was built in 1903 to accommodate the trains coming and going to Canada on the Atlantic and Saint Lawrence Railroad (taken over by the Grand Trunk Railroad), but was demolished in 1966 when rail passenger service ended. Note also the huge grain elevator that once stored Canadian wheat when Portland was Canada's ocean gateway during the winter months (when the St. Lawrence River was frozen). The Portland Company complex (just behind the elevator) was established in 1847 by John Poor, whose enthusiasm for railroads included building his own locomotives. He was instrumental in making Portland the winter port of Canada (see Appendix P, page 190.) To convince the Canadian government to ship its grain to Portland instead of the competing Boston, Poor traveled alone by sleigh in a blinding blizzard in February 1845 to Montreal, where, at the last moment, he was able to convince the Canadians to award the contract to Portland. He later wrote:

"I was happily met with an attentive reaction
and the idea seemed to take full possession of
several number of the Board that any other Route
than that of Portland would fail to secure to Montreal
the great advantage of the trade of the St. Lawrence
Valley."

The Grand Trunk office building at One India Street is all that remains today of a once imposing complex. Fore Street, which winds its way on the left side of the picture up to the Eastern Promenade, was once at the water's edge, until Commercial Street was built in 1851 by filling in part of the harbor. Thus, everything to the right of Fore Street as shown here would have been covered by the waters of Casco Bay had the photograph been taken prior to 1851. The train station, the tracks, the elevator, and the Portland Company are all built on man-made land, hallmarks of the coming of the industrial age to Portland.

Chapter Three – The Old Port and Waterfront

Mainers have a long history of entrepreneurial activity, and it has always been in their cultural makeup to be self-sufficient and enterprising. Leon Bean started his world-famous company in 1912 in a twenty-five-by-forty basement room and a small, rented store in Freeport. The Cianchette brothers founded Cianbro Construction Company in 1949 with an old truck and some savings from their stints in the army. And like these legendary entrepreneurs, Arthur Hannaford's supermarket chain began in 1883 when he delivered fresh produce in a one-horse cart from this store on lower Market Street in Portland (that's him in the middle cart with the white horse.) The Hannafords were farmers in Cape Elizabeth, and Arthur opened this waterfront shop as an outlet for the produce they grew on the farm. The business prospered, and in 1902 Howard and Edward Hannaford joined Arthur, and together they incorporated the Hannaford Brothers Company. From these humble beginnings in Portland's Old Port, Hannaford now operates 171 stores in Maine, New Hampshire, Vermont, Massachusetts and New York.

The Portland Yacht Club built at Central Wharf in 1885

The Portland Yacht Club has an interesting history. First organized in 1869, it built this clubhouse on the end of Central Wharf in 1885. This first clubhouse burned in 1926 and was replaced the following year by a lower building, designed by John Calvin Stevens, a yacht club member. It is this second building that most old-time Portlanders remember. Notice how, at this early date, many of the boats at the dock are small powerboats. As early as 1914, they outnumbered sailboats among yacht club members. (A rare photograph of the second clubhouse designed by John Calvin Stevens can be seen in Appendix F on page 180.)

In 1947, the club purchased property in Falmouth Foreside near the site of the old powerhouse that powered the electric trolley system (hence its address on Old Powerhouse Road.) It moved to its new facility in Falmouth later that year and has been located there ever since. Even though it was now located in Falmouth, it kept its original name (that it why it is called the Portland Yacht Club and not the Falmouth Yacht Club.) With all the changes to the Portland waterfront over the years, it was difficult to find this site of the original club, but it is given away by the Cumberland Cold Storage building on the right, seen in both photographs.

E. Swasey & Company Around 1900

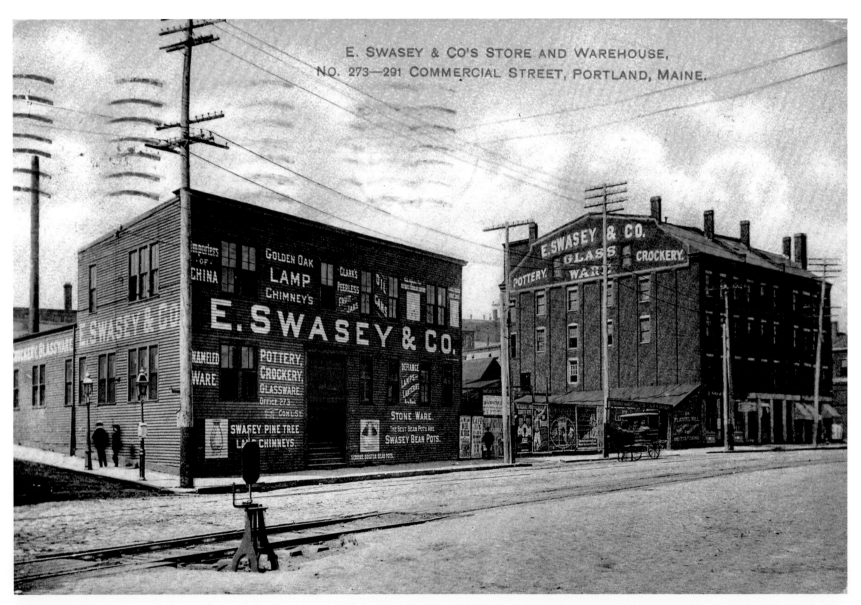

The City of Portland has always taken great pains to ensure its waterfront district would remain a working waterfront, with marine-related uses, as opposed to other commercial development, including the seemingly never-ending demand for more condominium units. The battle is not new. Even in the nineteenth century, along Commercial Street were non-marine-related businesses, like crockery dealers E. Swasey and Company. Its firm occupied a block between Center and Cross Streets. But a few blocks from the fire's origin, the brick building had escaped the 1866 conflagration and was enlarged the following year.

In the aftermath of the Great Fire, much blame was attributed to the city in its unpreparedness for such a calamity and its lack of an adequate water supply. *The Portland Advertiser* proclaimed: "The great desideratum was water. The wells and cisterns were drained early. Water, water, was the universal cry. The wall of fire walked on – no check anywhere. PORTLAND WAS DOOMED!" Today, the great desideratum is parking, as even one of the Swasey buildings shown opposite has given way to, you guessed it, another parking lot. Swasey's brick factory building still stands, however, converted to upscale condominium units.

This is the old Post Office, constructed at the corner of Middle and Exchange Streets of white Vermont marble between 1868 and 1871. Like the U.S. Custom House on Commercial Street, it was designed by U.S. Department of the Treasury architect Alfred B. Mullett (1834-1890). It stood on the same site as Portland's magnificent Exchange Building, lost tragically to fire in 1854 (see page 193 for more on the Exchange). This part of Exchange Street was first laid out in 1793, and was originally called Court Street. This is appropriate since the second floor of the old Post Office was used for United States court rooms and offices. The ornate building with its fine Corinthian columns served as Portland's main post office until the present one on Forest Avenue opened in 1934.

Today's Post Office Park is a far cry from what the square looked like when the Old Post Office was here. The Post Office stood for almost a century at the very heart of what had been the city of Portland's mercantile crossroads. Like the Union Station on the other side of town (lost in 1961), and John Bundy Brown's Falmouth Hotel (lost in 1963), the Post Office fell victim to a fit of urban renewal that swept Portland and many other cities in the 1960s. The refined civic building was leveled in 1965, initially for a parking lot, and more recently for the park seen here. Most now agree that the grandeur of Portland's built environment was greatly diminished by the loss of these landmark structures, once testimonials to Portland's prosperity, progress and civic pride.

Exchange Street Around 1890

If you have ever wondered what it was like to live in a world without cars, take a close look at this picture. We are standing at the intersection of Exchange Street and Middle Street, looking north toward Congress Street and City Hall. There are no cars in sight; everyone is riding a horse-drawn cart or carriage as they make their way about town. On the right above Middle Street is the old Post Office, its white Vermont marble standing out in sharp contrast to the warmer-colored brick buildings about it. On the left above Middle Street is the one-story wooden Fox Block, now demolished, which held many small shops.

At left is the 1867 Boyd Block, designed by George M. Harding. Today it is home to a popular Starbuck's Coffee store, with offices above. On the other side of Middle Street we can see where the Fox Block once stood on the left, and also where the old Post Office once stood on the right. Both buildings have been demolished and are now pocket parks, Tommy's Park on the left and Post Office Park on the right. At the end of Exchange Street is the new City Hall, built in 1909-12 to a design by the New York firm of Carrere and Hastings, with the assistance of John Calvin Stevens. Exchange Street is a popular tourist destination.

In 1952, the Portland City Council created the ominously named Slum Clearance and Redevelopment Authority. Its first move was to flatten a nine-block area between Middle and Fore Streets, although numerous legal challenges would delay the project for four years. When work finally began, entire blocks were knocked down, including both good and bad. The area, called Vine-Deer-Chatham, had been home to sixty-two families. Many of the residents were Italian-American and had lived there since their families had migrated from Italy many years earlier. Smack in the middle of this area, at the corner of Deer and Fore Streets, was this building, the former Curtis and Sons, which somehow escaped the destruction.

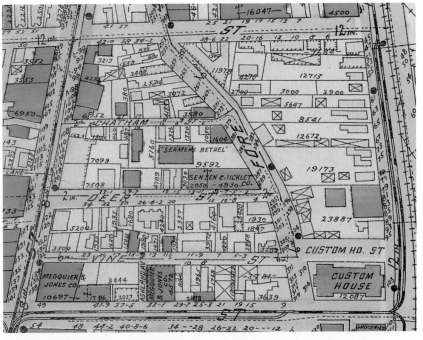

Street map of Vine-Deer-Chatham section of Portland, c. 1930

This five-story brick commercial block still stands at the corner of Fore and Deer Streets. Curtis and Sons was founded in 1850, and operated at this site from 1866 until 1920, making of all things Spruce gum, a product on which the company had a worldwide monopoly. At its height, the Curtis factory employed 200 people, mostly women, to make 1,800 boxes of chewing gum a day. Derived from Maine spruce trees, the once-popular product was sold throughout the United States, Canada, and Mexico. For the past few generations, this building of unusual shape has been owned by the Novick family, which operates the Hub Furniture Company there, as well as a small parking lot for patrons of the Old Port.

The Merchant's Bank and Board of Trade Building

Across the street from the Stanton Block, at 34 Exchange Street, stands the former Board of Trade Building, once occupied by the Merchant's National Bank. The Board of Trade had been incorporated in 1854:

.. to give tone and energy to the various branches of trade, and in securing the advantages which the position of the city offers to commerce and manufactures .... and where legislation is required in making such improvements, direct its efforts in a firm and vigorous manner .... so as to give the fullest development to all the natural advantages of the port, and provide for speedy and ample transportation of merchandise throughout the State .... to facilitate in every possible way encouragement of commerce, and to prevent discrimination to our disadvantage in the movement of merchandise on the sea, or on the land.

Its former headquarters on the same Exchange Street site was destroyed in the fire along with the original records. Early in 1868, the Board of Trade, the Merchants National Bank, the Bank of Portland and the National Traders Bank became co-tenants in the Matthew Stead-designed building.

In one of his walks about town, historian Edward Elwell writes as follows about the Board of Trade:

"On Exchange Street, opposite the entrance of Milk Street, our Board of Trade has its headquarters: an organization of our leading business men, which has done much to promote the prosperity of the city. Here also is the Merchants Exchange, with its reading room, whither our merchants resort for information, bargaining, and consultation. All who have an eye for fine architectural effects will admire the façade of the Merchants Bank on this street."

The bottom half of this building was actually painted white during the 1960s, when this and many other fine buildings on Exchange Street sat empty. Before it was restored in the 1970s, one observer remarked as follows:

"The contrast in requirements and public image between a business block and a banking structure is apparent. Horizontal breadth to accommodate store fronts gives way to a more architecturally formal design in this, the only stone building in a brick neighborhood. If the unfortunate and intrusive coat of white paint covering and visually severing the first story, were removed, and if the now lost roof line balustrade were replaced, this building's handsome arched rhythms would be more apparent. The alternation of large and small openings, single or clustered, the three bay definition by rusticated pilasters, the unusual shell motif in the second story windows and countless other decorative details, bespeak the aura of conservative prosperity so important to banks and boards of trade."

The Board of Trade Building has now been fully restored, and the results are dramatic. This has to be one of the most beautiful buildings in all of Portland. It is home today to a retail store on the ground floor, with office space above. At one point it risked a date with the wrecking ball, but luckily for us the building has survived.

Exchange Street was always known for printing of one kind or another, at least in the nineteenth century. On the upper part of Exchange, near the intersection with Federal Street, was ground zero for all the newspapers in town, and there were plenty. As historian Edward Elwell relates:

"Glancing up Exchange Street we see the fine block of the Portland Savings Bank, and not far above it the Printers Exchange, where are issued the Daily Argus (Democratic), the Daily Press (Republican), and several weekly newspapers, including Zion's Advocate (Baptist), and Christian Mirror. The Daily Advertiser is published at 197 Federal Street; the Portland Transcript (literary and family weekly), 44 Exchange; the Sunday Times (Independent), 31 Market; Portland Globe, 119 1/2 Exchange; Daily Morning News, corner Middle and Temple; City Item, 7 Exchange Street."

This particular building is at the very bottom of Exchange Street where it meets Fore Street, the ancient waterfront. We see from the photograph that it is home to M.N. & F.G. Rich Printers. Also sharing the building is the International Telegraph Company and Henry F. Wood, Stock and Specie Broker. There is also the Independent Insurance Agency and, on the ground floor on Exchange Street, John E. Dow and Sons. Judging from the pile of rocks on the corner, it would appear that the cobblestones were in the midst of being replaced when this photograph was taken.

Anyone who frequents Portland's Old Port today will immediately recognize this building as the home of Bull Feeney's Bar and Grill at the corner of Exchange Street and Fore Street. While Bull Feeney's entrance is actually to the right of this building in the former Seaman's Club, the top floors have been extended into this building, making for a large establishment with lots of room to roam about and enjoy a drink or two with your friends. On the ground floor is a variety store, and depending on the time of year and who's leasing the space, a bar or two in the basement. The very top floor was recently used as a lawyer's office, and commands a wonderful view of the harbor. It may be used now as a private residence.

Exchange Street Around 1880

Here we have a wonderful shot of Exchange Street as it must have looked in its heyday during the 19th century. As indicated earlier, printers seem to have always done business here in one form or another, and this photograph reveals no exception. The Charles H. Ford Company is prominently advertising its printing service so that only a blind man could miss it; he does GOOD WORK at FAIR PRICES. On the left a horse and cart is either delivering a load or picking one up, and there are no cars in sight. Notice at the top of the hill the old Post Office on the right just beyond the Middle Street intersection.

Looking at the very same view today reveals much change to lower Exchange Street, which today has become a shopper's paradise, with retail shops of every description lining both sides of the street. We are standing here at the foot of Exchange Street looking up toward Middle Street. The former Rich's Printing Office (page 92) is on the immediate right. At the top of the hill, the space once occupied by the old Post Office is now a park, known in its honor as Post Office Park (the Post Office was regrettably torn down in 1965). Still, this neighborhood is very 19th century, and reminds one of Charles Dickens London.

Boothby Square Around 1902

This is a photograph of Boothby Square, a small park on Fore Street given to the city in 1902 by Col. Frederick E. Boothby. His gift included a granite water fountain for watering horses, that was years ago sold at auction to an antique dealer and only recently returned to the square. This view looking east from Market Street to Pearl Street includes a row of commercial buildings dating from 1792 to 1902. The Henry Goddard Block of 1831 is the last building on the right before the Custom House of 1868-71, shown in the distance. The buildings in the foreground have been replaced by the Evie Cianchette Block at right.

Before it was known as Boothby Square, this area was long known as Sailor Town because it was the haunt of sailors, stevedores and working men from Portland's waterfront. Prior to 1851, when Commercial Street was built on man-made land, this was the waterfront, and ships docked right up behind the row of buildings shown here. The four-story building on the right, at the intersection of Silver Street, was for years known as a brothel. The Silver House today is home to an art gallery, with modern apartments on the upper floors. The public sculpture *Tracing the Fore* in the middle of the square is widely regarded as a failure.

A Man and His Oxen on Fore Street Around 1890

This charming photograph shows a man and his oxen working the streets of Portland with a sled of some sort. Just exactly what he is doing is unknown. He has just left Boothby Square and is passing in front of the former Seaman's Club at 375 Fore Street. Designed and erected by Charles Quincy Clapp in 1866, the Seaman's Club features a remarkable set of windows on the second floor. These broad graceful Gothic lights feature four intertwining pointed arches topped by three medallions, all circumscribed by a gently rounded arch. This exquisite and broad expanse of windows anticipates later Victorian commercial facades. Notice the building on the right of the Seaman's Club. What were once gracefully arched ground floor windows have given way to 20th century picture windows.

A modern day photograph of the same scene shows a remarkably well preserved street front. At bottom right, Moulton Street comes up to meet Fore Street, while to the right is the entrance to Boothby Square. The building to the immediate right is the Fore Street side of the Mariner's Church, built in 1828-29 to provide for the religious edification of mariners. The merchant prince of Portland, Asa Clapp (1762-1848) was a shrewd investor who had a habit of buying up valuable properties in depressed markets. He owned this building once at a bargain price, before his descendant sold it in 1934 to the C.H. Robinson Company. Across the street is the entrance to Bull Feeney's, for years home to the Seaman's Club Restaurant and Bar, built, as mentioned, by Charles Clapp in 1866.

J.B. Brown's Falmouth Hotel (1867-68) on Middle Street, the "Hotel of a Thousand Banquets"

Edward Elwell writes eloquently about what he sees on the new, post-fire Middle Street. "All now before us, down Middle Street, is fresh and new. The fire of 1866 leveled everything here, and the new business structures which have arisen from the ruins far outshine the old in loftiness and architectural pretensions. Some are of brick covered with mastic; some of handsome pressed brick, with Albert-stone trimmings; others of Connecticut freestone, and some of granite, many having iron pillars, caps, sills, and ornamentations. The styles are various, and often ornate, the warerooms spacious and handsome. As far along here as the eye can sweep, the street architecture is of a noble and attractive character, the blocks of warehouses being diversified with hotels and bank buildings."

No building better symbolized the rebirth of Portland's commercial district after the 1866 fire than the Falmouth Hotel (opposite) at Middle and Union Streets. Erected in 1867-68 by J.B. Brown, the six-story Falmouth featured a grand sandstone façade and contained 240 guest rooms, a dining room, a billiard room, and 10 stores. Another victim of urban renewal, it was razed in 1963-64 after almost a century of service. Today, the site has been taken over by the new Key Bank Plaza, shown above, and serves as one of Portland's most distinguished office addresses. It is here that U.S. Senator Susan Collins maintains her Portland office, along with many other notable clients. (For more on the life of John Bundy Brown, see Appendix G on page 181.).

The U.S. Custom House on Commercial Street Around 1890, with barrels of fish on the way to market

The ashes of the Great Fire of 1866 were still smoldering when Portlanders turned to the hard task of rebuilding. Led by Mayor Augustus F. Stevens and his relief committee, everyone pitched in to help, and public construction kept pace with private initiative. A good example of this spirit is the new $485,000 granite custom house of 1868-72, designed by U.S. Treasury Department architect Alfred B. Mullett. Built near the waterfront between Pearl and Custom House Streets, the site slopes down from Fore Street to Commercial Street, allowing a full three-story principal façade on the waterfront with an equally handsome two-story façade on Fore Street. It is a far cry from the pine shed which had originally housed the Portland Collector of Customs. This image from about 1890 shows a caravan of wagons loaded with barrels of fish – haddock, cod, and mackerel – making its way along Commercial Street in front of the new custom house.

The building of Commercial Street along Portland's waterfront is itself an interesting story. The coming of the railroad to Portland in the 1840s spurred the city to undertake this enterprising scheme. To handle rail shipments more efficiently, the Atlantic & St. Lawrence Railroad, later taken over by the Grand Trunk, urged the city to fill in the waterfront below Fore Street, which had since earliest times followed the natural contours of the harbor and waterfront. This could link the Portland, Saco & Portsmouth terminal at the foot of High Street with that of the Atlantic & St. Lawrence near the foot of India Street. The city agreed and by 1853 Commercial Street, over a mile long and a hundred feet wide, with twenty-six feet in the center reserved for railroad tracks, was completed. The $80,000 expanse, lined with new warehouses and wharves, soon became the hub of Portland's booming import and export business, as it remains to this day.

Stephen Berry Printer at 37 Exchange Street Around 1890

The photograph on the left shows Stephen Berry, Printer, located at 37 Exchange Street, with a happy group of workers faithfully smiling for the camera in every window and door available. As noted earlier, it was always a special time when the cameraman showed up, with everyone scrambling to get into the picture. Whether this was pride of workmanship and one's place of employment, or just fascination with a new technology, we may never know. But people loved having their picture taken. The building at Number 37 Exchange Street has since been demolished. At right is the new 3-story building that replaced it.

Chapter Four – The West End and Deering

This remarkable aerial photograph of Portland's West End dates from around 1950, and reminds us of how much change has occurred in this section of Portland. Union Station is still alive and well at this date, although the era of the rail transportation was rapidly coming to a close. Built to service the Maine Central and Boston and Maine Railroads, it opened for business on June 25, 1888. By the 1960's it ran out of passengers, and trains, and it was closed on October 29, 1960, the victim of progress and the internal combustion engine. Sadly, the old station was demolished in 1961 and replaced by a shopping center. On the top of the hill we see the Bramhall-Vaughan Street reservoir. The area where it once stood is now a parking lot, one of many needed for the sprawling campus of the Maine Medical Center. In fact, the entire hill has now been taken over by the Maine Medical Center, shown as it looks today in Appendix T on page 194. Notice at left on Park Avenue the Portland Exposition Building, built in 1914 to address Portland's role as a growing convention center. Hadlock Stadium had not yet been built, and many of the functions of the "Expo" have now been taken over by the new Cumberland County Civic Center, built downtown in 1977.

Henley-Kimball Auto Dealership and Oakhurst Dairy on Forest Avenue

Used cars were purchased, sold, and exchanged at this lot on Forest Avenue around 1950. If you were in the market for a nice Hudson or Chrysler, you could probably find it here, on the Henley Kimball lot. In fact, Forest Avenue was where you went to find *any* car, as virtually all of the dealerships were located there. Notice, however, the Oakhurst Dairy building in the background. This family-owned and very successful dairy had an eye for expansion, and years later they acquired the Henley Kimball property to enlarge their dairy operations. If we could only go back in time and pluck a few of these vintage cars off the lot today!

Today, the car dealerships have all either relocated, or gone out of business, but the Bennett family's little dairy has kept on growing at this Forest Avenue location. Starting in 1921, Stanley T. Bennett delivered fresh milk to Portlanders in glass bottles by horse-drawn wagons. Ever since then, the story of Oakhurst Dairy has been one of growth, service, innovation, and success. In 1973, the dairy purchased the Henley Kimball lot and hasn't looked back. The dairy now occupies virtually the entire block from Falmouth Street to Bedford Street along Forest Avenue. And they still make the best chocolate milk in Portland!

Columbia Market on Forest Avenue

Old-time Portlanders will remember this place. This building at 334 Forest Avenue near Baxter Boulevard has seen many uses over the years, but in the early 1950s it was the home of Columbia Markets, which first incorporated in 1934. In recent years, this site was the home of Pier 1 Imports, with a bustling sports bar at the rear of the block patronized by many a University of Southern Maine student. Oakhurst Dairy, next door, has now expanded its property all the way from Falmouth Street right up to the edge of this building. In the background is the former Huston Biscuit Company, built at this location in 1919-20.

As of this writing, the former Columbia Market building was empty, looking for a new tenant. In the background, we can see many changes to the old Huston Biscuit Company building, designed by Webster and Libby and built here in 1919-20. Huston Biscuit Company was known as the "Baker of Better Biscuits since 1869". After being used by the National Biscuit Company, and later serving as a warehouse, the building was remodeled to become, beginning in 1993, one of the libraries of the University of Southern Maine. Shown next to it, today, is the new Osher Map Library.

Aerial View of the Deering Estate Around 1940

This aerial view of Portland from around 1940 shows the Deering Estate at center, flanked by Bedford Street running diagonally through the picture, and Forest Avenue along the top. At the very top we can see what Baxter Boulevard once looked like as it winds it way from Forest Avenue around the shores of Back Cove toward Payson Park and Washington Avenue on the opposite side of town. The Deering Estate land was purchased in 1946 by the Portland Junior College and is now home to the University of Southern Maine. Note all of the large three and four "flatter" homes in the neighborhood at right (Surrenden Street), and some undeveloped lots on Chamberlain Avenue. This entire area, or most of it, has now been taken over and developed by the University of Southern Maine.

An aerial view today reveals the extent of change that has occurred over the past 70 years. At right, Interstate 295 now cuts like a ribbon through the center of Portland, providing many exits to enter or leave the city from the suburbs nearby. The Huston Biscuit Company building was converted, starting in 1993, to the University's Glickman Library. More recent additions include the Osher Map Library where once stood Forest City Chevrolet (see page 250 and the preceding page). A huge parking garage now covers an entire block along Surrenden Street that once contained several homes. The entire Deering Estate has now been fully developed by the University, as have many homes in the surrounding neighborhoods. Note also the expansion of Oakhurst Dairy at the top of the picture.

A Gasoline Station on Forest Avenue

This is a wonderful photograph from the 1920s of a filling station on Forest Avenue whose location should be immediately apparent because of the building in the background. This particular station sold Maxher gasoline and Altex oil to keep the early Model Ts running smoothly and on the road, while behind the station looms the mighty T.A. Huston Company, "Baker of Better Biscuits Since 1869". Webster and Libby were the designers of Huston's new baking facility, which was built here quite near the Deering Estate in 1919-20. See also pages 114-115 for more views of this highly visible corner.

A recent photograph of the area taken from the same vantage point reveals the disappearance, long ago, of the two quaint filling stations that once occupied this site. They were a sign of the times while they lasted, just as the magnificent new Glickman Family Library is a sign of the times at today's campus of the University of Southern Maine. The renovation of the old Huston Biscuit Company building to become a library for the University began in 1993, and represents an excellent reuse of the property to fit contemporary needs. If only similar action had been taken to save Portland's Union Station or the old Post Office!

T.A. Huston & Company on Forest Avenue, "Baker of Better Biscuits Since 1869"

Long before it was a library for the University of Southern Maine, the building at the corner of Bedford Street and Forest Avenue was used for baking biscuits. This 1930s photograph gives a good view of the Huston Biscuit Company, also known by many as the Nabisco Building, which leased the property for many years. Of particular interest is the mixed use of the neighborhood at this time. Note on the corner the two small (and early) gas stations. Next to them, on Bedford Street, are two homes, just feet away from the Biscuit Company. Such things were common occurrences in an era before zoning laws.

A modern view of the same corner reveals much change. Gone are the days of pulling up here to gas up the old car. The filling stations are gone, and the homes in the neighborhood are gone. The only thing that remains is the surviving remnant of the Huston Biscuit Company, transformed starting in 1993, as if by magic, into the very modern looking Glickman Library of the University of Southern Maine. Next to it, and even more modern looking and more recent, is the Osher Map Library. Driving by this corner today one would hardly suspect that the area looked as it did seventy or eighty years ago.

Forest City Chevrolet in 1960

Most of the automobile dealerships in Portland were once located on Forest Avenue, or nearby, like this one – Forest City Chevrolet – at the intersection of Bedford and Winslow Streets. The photograph was taken in July of 1960, and shows the dealer's lineup of brand new 1960 Chevys. Whether you wanted a sedan, a coupe or even a station wagon, you could find it here. Notice in the background of this picture the seven-story Nabisco Building, which at this time was still used for baking biscuits. Years later, when the University took over this site, the dealership building was used as headquarters for the campus police.

In the preceding photograph, Winslow Street is shown angling off to the right of Bedford Street. This was a short, dead-end street that was totally obliterated when the Osher Map Library was built. The entrance to the library's parking lot shown here is the closest remnant we have left of what was once Winslow Street. Today, Forest City Chevrolet is still very much in business, but has moved across town to a new location on Brighton Avenue, near the Pine Tree Shopping Center. Where it once stood is now home to a magnificent complex of library buildings of the University of Southern Maine.

Portland Airport in 1948

This is a view of the Portland Municipal Airport as it appeared in 1948, just after World War II. The same terminal building can still be seen in the background, and the airport was still very small in scale, as the incoming planes simply pulled up to the terminal building and let you off. At the time this photograph was taken, Eastern Airlines was the primary carrier of most flights into and out of Portland. Note the propellers on the airplane. Though jets existed in 1948, the technology was still very much in its infancy, as the United States captured German aircraft at war's end and then refined the technology here.

This is a similar view of the former terminal building in a contemporary photograph of the Maine Aviation building at the Portland International Jetport (PWM). From this vantage point, you can see that the building is the same one as in the earlier photograph taken in 1948. Note, for example, the right wing of the building that is visible under the nose of the airplane in the picture on the preceding page. All that is missing in this current view are the beautiful elm trees seen in the earlier photograph. PWM, in case you ever wondered when checking your bags, stands for Portland Westbrook Municipal. Now you know!

There are lots of photographs of Portland's Union Station, but none better than this one, taken shortly after the station closed on October 29, 1960. The image was captured by James Lekousi, owner of Lekousi's Bakery on Congress Street, between Valley and St. John, from the roof top of his bakery building. Designed by the Boston firm of Bradlee, Winslow, and Wetherell, the Romanesque Revival Union Station was a building of exceptional architectural merit that opened for business on June 25, 1888 to serve the Boston and Maine and Maine Central Railroads. Sadly, it was demolished in 1961 to make way for a new shopping center.

As stunned onlookers gathered to watch, the tower of Portland's magnificent Union Station came crashing to the ground on August 31, 1961. It was the end of an era. Boston real estate developer Samuel W. Poorvu had purchased the former train terminal from the Portland Terminal Company for $250,000, and after tearing down the building, established this 12-acre shopping center on the site. It was home for years to Arlan's Department Store, with a First National Grocery Store at the far end. Its disappearance heralded the beginning of the historic preservation movement. (See Appendix H on page 182 for more.)

View of Union Station from Western Promenade

This is an interesting photograph of Union Station taken from the vantage point of the Western Promenade. We know that the station was lengthened in 1906, so the picture must have been taken prior to that time, as the addition does not appear. In the foreground we can see many of the homes on Valley Street, just below Bramhall's Hill, but worlds away from the mansions lining the Western Promenade at the top of the hill. At the very left we can see the edge of the Maine Central Office Building, which was not completed until 1916. Also of note, in the distance are many homes of the Libbytown neighborhood, now gone.

The very same scene today shows many changes to this West End neighborhood. To get your bearings, look at the white home in the center of this photograph, the one with the dormered roof, and compare it to the same building in the earlier photograph. The only change is the dormer that has been added. The buildings in the foreground of the earlier view on Valley Street are no longer there, and of course the biggest change is the Union Station itself, demolished in 1961 to make way for the shopping center we see today. The Cumberland County Jail complex, which replaced the Monroe Street jail, is visible in the background.

Railroad Crossing on Read Street

Talk about the perfect job, take a look at these guys! As the use of the automobile increased, railroads had to keep up with things by installing and manning more railroad barriers in certain locations. About a mile north of the Woodfords station, Read Street crosses the Maine Central Railroad tracks. Because the automobile's noisy engines made it hard for a driver to hear approaching trains, there was more need for barriers at railroad crossings without clear views, like this one; and those barriers had to be hand operated. It must have been a great job, as these men do not appear to be overly stressed out by the work.

Chapter Four: The West End and Deering

One look at the same Read Street location reveals how much things have changed over the past fifty years. Gone are the days of men sitting at a railroad crossing waiting to manually lower the barrier whenever a train went by. That task was automated many years ago. We can also see from this picture that where there were once two and three sets of railroad tracks, there is now only a single track, evidence of how much the railroad business has shrunk from busier times during the heyday of railroad transportation. The old crossing shed has been demolished; trees have been cleared to make way for a new factory building.

The Forest City Diner on St. John Street

This will be a familiar sight to anyone who ever visited, or perhaps grew up on, Portland's West End. The Forest City Diner was located on St. John Street just across from the Union Station, and was at the time one of several diners in the city. Its chief competitor was the Miss Portland Diner, located across town on Forest Avenue just below the Post Office. After being moved to a new site on Marginal Way, the Miss Portland Diner continued in service from 1949, when it opened, until 2004, when the owner retired. After being donated to the city, it has now re-opened under new ownership at a new site on Marginal Way.

The Forest City Diner was not to be so lucky. Soon after the demolition of Portland's Union Station, the diner also went out of business and was either relocated elsewhere or demolished. In its place today is a d'angelos sandwich shop, at this location of St. John Street for the past several years. Notice the Maine General Hospital building on the top of the hill in both pictures. In an era when the City of Portland has seen so much change, in such a relatively short span of years, it is nice to consider the interest shown by the city in saving the Miss Portland Diner. The citizens of Portland should be proud to have at least one good diner left.

Cobblestones Being Laid at Bramhall Square

This has got to be one of the best photographs in this entire book! Shown on a stretch of Congress Street at Bramhall Square are a dozen or so men, sitting on the ground, and getting ready to lay new cobblestones on the street. This had to be back-breaking work, and this perhaps accounts for the posture of the men. The photograph appears to be before the advent of the automobile, so can probably be reliably dated to about 1900. As with so many other photographs from this era, the men all seem quite happy to have their picture taken, their work memorialized for all time to come with the snap of a shutter.

Looking at the exact same view of Congress Street today, the most obvious change is the fact that the streets are no longer paved with cobblestones. Most of the buildings visible in the earlier photo are still standing, including the one at the left, which is the five-story Maine Eye and Ear Infirmary of 1891-92. Erected at the corner of Congress and Vaughan Streets, this was a medical facility for Dr. Eugene Holt, a noted authority on eye and ear diseases. It was designed by John Calvin Stevens in an eclectic blend of Romanesque and Colonial Revival styles. After many decades of medical service, it was converted to apartments in 1998.

This is a great early photograph of the Maine General Hospital. In 1868 plans were drafted for the hospital to be built on the site of the state arsenal on Bramhall Hill. Portlanders raised $100,000 toward its construction through sales, fairs, and donations. Construction began in 1871, and the east wing of this modern facility with its lovely view of the White Mountains was accepting patients by 1874. Designed in the High Victorian Gothic style by Francis H. Fassett, the building was based on state-of-the-art hospitals in Boston and New York. The entire hospital with west wing and central pavilion was finally completed in 1892.

Today's Maine Medical Center complex was built in stages around a central core of the old Maine General Hospital, shown here still standing at the heart of the complex, but used now for administrative offices rather than for patient care. When it opened, Maine General Hospital was a 40-bed facility that served 114 patients. In 1951, it merged with the Maine Eye and Ear Infirmary (1892) and the Children's Hospital (1908) to become the Maine Medical Center. A series of construction projects, including a $46 million expansion in 1984, has created the present-day complex of more than a million square feet. (See also page 194.)

On the left, Maine Central train E-7 709 awaits departure from Union Station on June 29, 1955. The days of rail travel were rapidly coming to an end, a victim of progress and the internal combustion engine. As the use of automobiles proliferated, and trucks began carrying goods nationwide with more convenience and less cost (especially after the interstate highway system was built in the late 1950s), people no longer needed or used trains. Rather than seek an alternative use of the property, it was sold and demolished. On the right, we see the back side of the shopping center that was built to replace the station. A few tracks are left.

Chapter Five – Parks and Bridges

Most of this book has been about buildings, but there are other structures, and places, that figure in a region's history. In this chapter, we explore the parks and bridges that have made Portland, and continue to make it, an interesting place to live. Shown above is a view of the so-called Million Dollar Bridge that spanned the Fore River between Portland and South Portland for nearly a century. Nicknamed for its price tag, the Million Dollar Bridge was built to provide a more convenient path to the Portland waterfront from the Knightville section of South Portland. Permits to construct the bridge were issued by the Secretary of War in 1893, but several years elapsed while financing was put in place. Designed in 1914, construction got under way soon thereafter, and the bridge finally opened to traffic in 1916. This view shows a trolley car crossing the bridge on its way to South Portland. Notice how the bridge was high enough on the Portland side to take traffic above Commercial Street. Though some may debate the point, this bridge was arguably much more beautiful than the one that replaced it.

Since colonial times, several spans have connected Sandy Point on the tip of Munjoy Hill to Seacomb's Point on the East Deering shore. In 1791, private citizens formed a corporation to build a bridge, thus eliminating an arduous land journey of five or six miles to get to the opposite shore a few hundred feet away. The officially named Back Cove Bridge opened in 1796 as a toll bridge, but the popular mind called it after the tolltaker Lemuel Tukey, a name it retains to this day. By 1830 people had tired of paying the toll and called for a free bridge. An agreement was reached whereby the city would repair the bridge and the owners would continue to charge tolls until their expenses were met. By 1837, the city decided the expenses had been met, but some proprietors thought otherwise. One stout owner posted himself at the gate and continued to charge. It took a mob of Back Cove men, who threw the gate into the sea and threatened to do the same with the proprietor, to accomplish the freeing of Tukey's bridge. Shown above is Tukey's Bridge viewed from the Eastern Promenade ca. 1900.

This modern view of Tukey's Bridge taken from the trail below the Eastern Promenade shows a scene much different from a century earlier. Long gone is the business shown next to the bridge that made Wiley's Waxene and William Tell flour. Today's structure is also much higher than its predecessor, and is now part of Interstate 295 as it winds its way through the city. It is interesting to note that Back Cove was once an important commercial inlet for Portland. According to William Willis, "Large quantities of wood cut in town, and some of it upon the Neck as late as the Revolution, were sent to Boston, the vessels frequently going round Back Cove and up Wear Creek which empties into it, to receive their cargoes." In the age of sail, rope making was another important industry, and the largest of Portland's four major rope walks – Hammond's – was accessed via the cove. Looking at today's Hammond Street, which evolved from the rope walk, it is hard to believe that the waters of Back Cove once touched it. Only kayakers and windsurfers go under Tukey's Bridge today!

The basics of Portland's transportation systems were in place by the 1880s. Most streets had been laid out, if not entirely built up, including Commercial Street, on filled land at the edge of the harbor, and others on fill at the head of Back Cove. Bridges united the peninsula with neighboring areas. Indeed, fill had made some of them more causeways than bridges. Five different rail lines came into the city; and other rails had been laid for a system of horse-drawn streetcars. Pictured here is Vaughan's Bridge, first built in 1800 and named for its major proponent, William Vaughan. It was rebuilt a few times, including in 1913 – about when this photograph was taken – and replaced in the early 1950s by the Veterans Memorial Bridge. It carried traffic from Cassidy point to South Portland.

William Vaughan (1745-1826) was a wealthy merchant who, to increase the value of his 400 acre holdings on the Western Promenade, promoted the building of Vaughan's Bridge (opened in 1800) and laid out Bridge Street (now part of Danforth) to connect it with the town. Unfortunately for Vaughan, the Embargo Act of 1807 ruined Portland's commerce and his fortune vanished, his lands taken by creditors. As Willis notes: "His conceptions were right, as our present experience proves, but his visions were premature, he was two-thirds of a century in advance of his time." Today William Vaughan is memorialized by Vaughan Street and the house he built at 387 Danforth Street in 1799. The bridge he built no longer exists, other than a single remaining piece of hand rail shown above.

The Veterans Memorial Bridge was constructed in 1953 to replace the aging Vaughan's Bridge, which started out from the Portland shore just around the corner from here at Cassidy's Point and spanned the Fore River, connecting Portland to South Portland via busy U.S. Route 1. In this photograph, a workman is shown sitting atop one of the piers of the new bridge as it was being constructed. The railroad tracks shown sweeping across the river and under the bridge are part of the Boston and Maine system bringing trains from Boston to Portland's Union Station, which was located on St. John Street about a mile from here. When it was completed, the new Veterans Memorial Bridge also carried traffic to Route 1 in South Portland.

The Veterans Memorial Bridge is slated for replacement in 2010. The 56-year-old bridge carries 23,000 cars per day, and the decking on it and the pilings are deteriorating, as can be partially seen in this photograph. The Maine Department of Transportation (MDOT) and Portland Area Comprehensive Transportation System (PACTS) have been working with both cities and stakeholders to develop a plan for a new bridge. Greater Portland Landmarks and the Portland Society of Architects are advocating for design excellence for this important gateway to the community. A major concern is how to link Portland's west end, South Portland's Ligonia neighborhood (originally named for Sir Fernando Gorges' mother, Cecily Lygon) and the Maine Mall area for cyclists and walkers.

Envisioned by Mayor James Phinney Baxter (1831-1921) in the 1890s, a boulevard was constructed around the shore of Back Cove in 1916-17. Baxter had lobbied hard for the non-profit development of the whole Back Cove area. In 1896, the Olmstead Brothers of Boston were commissioned to plan the roadway around the Cove, and though opened in 1916-17, land acquisition continued until 1932. Linking Forest Avenue to Washington Avenue, the two-and-one-quarter-mile roadway helped to open the Deering suburbs to residential development and provided a beautiful drive from which to view the city. This particular view was used on a postcard, and by the looks of things it must have been designed by a British firm; the automobile shown is driving on the wrong side of the road!

Today's boulevard is as beautiful as ever. The part originally called Back Cove Boulevard was renamed Baxter Boulevard in 1921, the year of the former mayor's death. During his six terms as mayor, Portland businessman, historian, and philanthropist James P. Baxter worked tirelessly for improvements to the city's parks as well as for creation of the boulevard that bears his name. He hired the Olmstead Brothers of Boston to plan the course of the road, and at his own expense took the city council to Boston to study its promenades and parks. He also negotiated with landowners around the Cove and convinced them to relinquish a one-hundred foot strip of land, reassuring them that the proposed boulevard would improve the value of their properties. And so it has!

Fort Allen Park

To enhance the Eastern Promenade, Portland created Fort Allen Park in 1890. This was originally the four-and-a-half-acre site of artillery batteries erected in the Revolutionary War and the War of 1812 to protect the town from British invasion. The original fort was rebuilt in 1814 and named in memory of Commander William Henry Allen. The main mast and navigational bridge and shield of the naval cruiser "U.S.S. Portland", a World War II ship, is in the park. Also in the park is a gun from the battleship "Maine". Note in this photograph from about 1895 the three-and four-masted schooners that were once anchored in the harbor.

On Munjoy Hill, one can go to Fort Allen Park, stand on the embankments of the old fort, and look out at Longfellow's islands, so called, – the islands that Longfellow loved as a boy and wrote about in his poem *My Lost Youth*: "I can see the shadowy lines of its trees,/ And catch, in sudden gleams,/ The sheen of the far-surrounding seas,/ And islands that were the Hesperides/ Of all my boyish dreams." The islands in Casco Bay that Longfellow saw from here were the Diamond Islands, Peaks Island, House Island and Cushing Island. And just as for Longfellow, they remain an inspiration for all who view them today!

View of Western Promenade from Maine General Hospital

The Western Promenade was laid out in 1837 as the west end counterpart to the Eastern Promenade. The new promenade afforded views of the Maine countryside all the way to the White Mountains in New Hampshire. This view from the early 20th century shows the Western Promenade as seen from the tower of the Maine General Hospital (today's Maine Medical Center). It featured lush plantings, sidewalks, and visible in this photograph, the shingled bandstand designed by John Calvin Stevens and Albert Winslow Cobb in 1890, now lost (see page 158 for the Eastern Promenade counterpart, recently restored).

Mayor James P. Baxter's most praiseworthy contribution to Portland was the part he played in creating the city's park system. When he was first elected in 1893, he dreamed of ringing the city with green tree-shaded areas, and worked tirelessly during his six terms of office to make his dream a reality. One of the things he did as mayor was arrange the exchange with the J.B. Brown heirs of a piece of city-owned land for their land on the northwestern slopes of the Western Promenade. Portlanders owe much to this great man. The tower of the old Maine General Hospital, shown here, is now closed, but the view is still spectacular!

Eastern Promenade Around 1920

Portland's first public land was acquired on Munjoy Hill in 1828 and contributed in 1837 to the formation of the Eastern Promenade, a tree-lined drive extending from Fore Street to Washington Avenue. In this view from the 1920s, we are looking south toward Fort Allen Park, where the promenade is lined with large two-and-three family homes overlooking the island-studded waters of Casco Bay. As with so many other parts of Portland, large, graceful elm trees once arched above the road here to provide a shaded oasis of beauty and calm. Sadly, they were lost to disease in the 1960s. The view, however, remains as beautiful as ever.

With the exception of the loss of the magnificent elm trees in the 1960s, very little has changed along Portland's Eastern Promenade. Many of the larger homes that were once single family residences have been converted to two-and-three family homes today, while others have been given over to condominiums, but they still grace the view here, and lucky indeed are the few who can afford to call this place their home. With its panoramic views of Portland Harbor and the islands of Casco Bay, the Eastern Promenade continues to command one of the best vantage points anywhere in the state from which to see Maine's fabled ocean.

This view of Portland's Eastern Promenade is looking north toward Tukey's Bridge (visible at right) and East Deering. Noticeably absent along this stretch of the promenade are the large homes that were built up on the southern end, providing a beautiful and secluded place to walk and to enjoy the many fine views to be had here. One of the most distinctive features of both the Eastern and Western Promenades were the large elm trees that once lined the sidewalks, but which were lost to disease in the 1960s. Still, there are very few places anywhere on earth to compare with the views here. This is one of Portland's real treasures!

Driving or walking down this stretch of Portland's Eastern Promenade is still a treat, more than 170 years after it was first laid out. Surprisingly, not everyone was in favor of the plan. When the Eastern and Western Promenades were first laid out in 1836, the *Eastern Argus* noted, "They may be very pleasant for those that keep horses and gig and have nothing to do but ride about, but they will not be the least advantage to nine-tenths of the taxpayers of the city." Luckily for present-day Portlanders, this sentiment was not widely shared, and the promenades were created the following year.

Lincoln Park

Created as a firebreak between the old and newly rebuilt sections of the city after the Great Fire of 1866, Lincoln Park occupies the block surrounded by Congress, Pearl, Federal and Franklin Streets (now Franklin Arterial). The two-and-a-half-acre section of land was once closely covered with older, smaller buildings, but was condemned after the fire and turned into Phoenix Park, a reference to the mythical bird that rose from the ashes, just as Portland had. After the Civil War, the park was renamed in honor of President Abraham Lincoln. The land was purchased for only $81,534; at 75 cents a square foot, a real bargain.

Here we see Lincoln Park as it appears on Congress Street today. For such a dense city, there is an unusual amount of open space in Portland, thanks largely to the foresight of those who planned parks, like this one, in the nineteenth century. Lincoln Park, originally laid out after the fire as a safety measure, is a large, shady area which also offers a refreshing counterpoint to the abutting government buildings. It was added to the National Register of Historic Places in 1989. Boothby Square, Monument Square and Longfellow Square also provide punctuation to the bustle of the city, as do the historic Eastern and Western Cemeteries.

Entrance Deering Park, Portland, Me.

66436

Deering Oaks is a 46 acre park that Portland acquired from the Deering heirs in 1879 in exchange for a tax abatement agreement with the family. This remarkable bargain gave the city a public breathing space in the spirit of New York City's Central Park. It is the largest parkland connected to the peninsula. Shown here are the stately granite pillars which have graced the Park Avenue entrance to Deering Oaks since 1902-04, designed by Frederick A. Tompson (1857-1906). They were once surmounted with two highly ornamental electrical globes believed to have been fabricated in Chicago, but now lost.

Ask yourself how many times you have driven through Deering Oaks and never noticed these wonderful entrance columns designed by Frederick A. Tompson. In the year they were installed, 1904, State Street was widened to accommodate the increasing horse-drawn as well as horseless traffic. By 1918, the increasing volume of auto traffic led to more roadway improvements and the addition of street lights on State Street. More than 60 years later, in 1980, lighting was installed throughout the interior of Deering Oaks. It is estimated to cost $150,000 to replace the two electrical globes that once sat atop these granite columns.

The Duck House at Deering Oaks Park

An enduring landmark at Portland's Deering Oaks Park enjoyed by generations of citizens over the years is the Duck House in the middle of the pond. In 1887, City civil engineer William A. Goodwin constructed a riprap island to accommodate a wooden model of a stylish Queen Anne residence, built by the Legrow Brothers Lumber Company as part of its float in the 1886 Portland Centennial Parade. Shown above in a photograph from the early 20th century is the original Legrow Brothers structure. Today, a modified version of the Duck House still shelters the park's waterfowl during the summer months. Talk about easy living!

If not for the red paint on this Queen Anne-style replica, it would be difficult to tell this house from the original Duck House built by the Legrow Brothers for the 1886 Portland Centennial Parade. For over a century, the Duck House has delighted visitors to Deering Oaks Park and created fond memories of the type written about by Henry Wadsworth Longfellow in his poem *My Lost Youth*: "And Deering's Woods are fresh and fair,/ And with joy that is almost pain/ My heart goes back to wander there,/ And among the dreams of the days that were,/ I find my lost youth again." Who can visit this park today and not feel youthful again?

A shelter for humans was built on the shore of Deering Oaks's pond in 1894. The picturesque, towered, Queen Anne-style brick and granite building contained an ornamental fireplace at which skaters could warm themselves on winter afternoons. Designed by Frederick A. Tompson (1857-1906), Portland's Castle in the Park has recently been restored to its original appearance. Note in the background of this early 20th century photograph the power station on Forest Avenue which once powered the city's electric trolley system. Until the late 1990's, paddle boats like the one shown above could be rented during the summer months.

This photograph shows the recently restored Queen Anne-style Castle in the Park designed by Frederick A. Tompson in 1894. Many a Portlander can remember days from their youth spent skating on the pond during Maine's notoriously long and cold winter months, thankful to have a warm place with a roaring fire from which to escape the icy cold. The paddle boats seen in the previous photograph are no longer available to rent. They were once a favorite means to explore the confines of the pond during the warm summer months, as well as a great way to enjoy the scenery in this beautiful park located in the midst of the busy city.

Here we see two views of the shingled bandstand designed by the architects John Calvin Stevens and Albert Winslow Cobb for Fort Allen Park in 1890. As originally planned, Fort Allen Park was designed to enhance the Eastern Promenade with its breathtaking views of Portland Harbor, and the bandstand made the park a more interesting place to visit, especially when a gathering was planned and rain threatened. A similar bandstand was also designed by Stevens and Cobb for the Western Promenade, but is now lost. The photograph on the right shows the recently restored Eastern Promenade bandstand, virtually a carbon copy of the original, and now used for the popular "Summer in the Parks" concert series sponsored by the Portland Recreation and Facilities Department and local area businesses. The photograph on the left shows the original bandstand as it looked shortly after the park was opened in 1890. Perhaps with a renewed effort by caring citizens and some philanthropic giving by a generous donor, we may one day see the other bandstand on the Western Promenade restored to its original location. Lovers of the "Summer in the Parks" concert series will enjoy "Nostalgia Nights" at the Fort Allen bandstand, which features the music of the popular Chandler's Band, the second oldest continuing community band in the nation.

Chapter Six – Around Town

According to a recent report commissioned by the Maine Office of Tourism, the Greater Portland region receives over 13.5 million visitors per year. In order of preference, these visitors like to shop (especially at the L.L. Bean store in Freeport), try local foods, including fresh Maine lobster, visit historic areas, and see the ocean. This chapter looks at some of the interesting sights that are but a short drive from Portland, starting with the small town of Freeport just a few miles north of the city, where the L.L. Bean store is located. Pictured above is Freeport Square as it appeared around 1912, the year that Leon Leonwood Bean (1872-1967) opened his famous store in that town. His original store was located in the Libby Block shown here on the right. Later, as demand for his product grew and the small store became insufficient for his needs, he moved across the street to the Warren Block, just above the Freeport Post Office, on the left. There were no outlet stores or tour buses operating in Freeport at this early date, just a set of solitary trolley tracks running down the middle of the street, and a few local residents walking along the sidewalks. The great era of mass merchandising was about to begin. For more on the life of L.L.Bean, see Appendix L on page 186.
.

The Portland sugar baron John Bundy Brown (1805-1881) came to Portland penniless and eventually became a leading industrialist and the city's largest landowner. Brown was a savvy real estate investor, and for his own home he built "Bramhall", an imposing villa between the Western Promenade and Vaughan Street, and developed the surrounding land into the city's most beautiful residential area. Built between 1855 and 1858 to a design by Charles A. Alexander, the estate covered nearly ten acres of prime land overlooking the promenade with beautiful views to the west of the White Mountains in New Hampshire. When it was demolished around 1915, the Bramhall Estate was subdivided into individual house lots for the rich and famous, including several members of the Brown family and their spouses. The one estate covered the area in present-day Portland bordered by Bowdoin Street, Vaughan Street, Pine Street and the Western Promenade, four entire city blocks that became the new home to roughly fifty or so houses, many designed by the prominent Portland architect John Calvin Stevens (1855-1940). This photograph shows one of the side entrances to the estate, complete with granite columns and wrought-iron entrance gates made by the Portland Company. Though the estate is now gone, the columns and entrance gates have survived, and now mark the entrance to Thornhurst Road in Falmouth Foreside. Notice the letter "B" in the gates, standing for "Bramhall". (For more on the Bramhall Estate, see Appendix G on page 181. For more on the Thornhurst Estate, see Appendix I on page 183.)

After the Civil War, one of John Bundy Brown's sons, Portland banker General John Marshall Brown (1838-1907) established Thornhurst Farm in Falmouth on a narrow point of land between two coves. Thornhurst Road gave access to the property, upon which was constructed a 22-room summer cottage designed by John Calvin Stevens (see Appendix I on page 183 for more on the Thornhurst Estate). When "Bramhall" was demolished and divided into lots, one of the first homes to be built there in 1906 was that of the Portland banker Herbert Payson (1860-1940), who had married Gen. Brown's daughter Sally Carroll Brown (1867-1948). Shortly thereafter, the original granite columns and entrance gates to Bramhall were moved to Thornhurst Road in Falmouth, where they survive to this day. It may have been Sally Carroll who moved them there. Her son, Henry Payson Jr., inherited the Thornhurst Estate upon Mrs. Brown's death in 1948. Notice the letter "B" in the middle of the gate, which stands for Bramhall.

The Town Landing Market in Falmouth Around 1915

This is a wonderful photograph of the Town Landing Market in Falmouth Foreside, taken around 1915. Filling up at the local Socony gas station, or filling station as they were then called, are some early Model T Fords. The Standard Oil Company of New York, or Socony, was one of the 34 new companies formed when Standard Oil was dissolved in 1911 by the Justice Department. Over the past 125 years, the building housing the Town Landing Market has served as a tearoom, a restaurant, an ice-cream parlor, and a gas station. At the time this picture was taken, it was called Calden's Ice Cream Parlor and gasoline station.

Today, the Town Landing Market in Falmouth continues its long service to visiting boaters, tourists, and local area neighborhood residents, who visit the store for a morning paper, fresh fruit and seafood, homemade pies, an Italian sandwich, beer, wine, or just about anything else, including gossip. The store's owner since 1981, Dan Groves is also a lobsterman, bringing back a fresh supply of the tasty crustaceans daily to the store, which serves the best lobster roll to be had anywhere in the State of Maine. The colorful sign outside the store advertises "Fresh Native Ice Cubes", adding to the charm of this local landmark.

Barracks at Fort McKinley, 1917

Built between 1891 and 1907 on the northeast end of Great Diamond Island, Fort McKinley was designed to defend Portland harbor during the Spanish-American war. Manned in peacetime as well as during wars, it housed more than 1,000 soldiers in brick barracks (like this one) and Queen Anne-style officers' quarters surrounding a stately parade ground. It was deactivated in 1945 at the close of World War II, languished unoccupied for more than 30 years, and developed into a residential community in the 1980's. In August 1917, a soldier sent this card to an acquaintance saying it was "the barracks we stay in".

Here is the same building almost a century after the postcard was sent. Though most of Fort McKinley has been redeveloped into a very fine residential community known as Diamond Cove, this double barracks on the property has been left to deteriorate, so much so that a tree is actually growing directly out of the concrete steps! In 2007, the Diamond Cove Homeowners Association voted to turn the barracks into 20 condominium/hotel units to be known as The Inn at Diamond Cove. The planned $10 million project has been held up in litigation, however, by island residents who oppose it, with resolution expected in 2010.

The story of Portland Breakwater Light starts in 1831, when a massively destructive storm wrecked most of Portland Harbor, flooding the Cumberland and Oxford Canal, ripping ships from their moorings, and partially destroying Vaughan's Bridge. The recommended solution was to build a 2,500 foot-long breakwater at Stanford Point in South Portland using 50,000 cubic yards of stone and rubble from nearby islands. Construction began in 1835, and by 1837 the breakwater was 1,765 feet long. In 1855, a wooden, octagonal light tower was built twenty-five feet over high tide. In cold winter weather, the breakwater's rubble became icy and difficult to maneuver without slipping. Keepers were often reduced to crawling the entire length of the breakwater during winter storms to prevent falling into Portland Harbor. In 1872, a handrail was added to mitigate the hazardous task of getting to and from the tower, and the breakwater was reinforced with 2,750 tons of new granite. (To see a picture of the original wooden light tower built here in 1855, see Appendix J on page 184, upper left.)

In 1872, the original wooden tower was replaced with a new 13 foot cast-iron tower modeled after the Greek Choragic Monument of Lysicrates and cast by the Portland Company (see Appendix J on page 184 for more on the Choragic Monument). Its seams are disguised by six decorative Corinthian columns. The architect was Thomas Ustick Walter (1804-1887), best known as the designer of the U.S. Capitol east and west wings and its current dome. A two-room wooden keeper's house was erected next to the tower in 1889, while other rooms were added incrementally as needed. The house was actually wider than the breakwater and overhung Portland Harbor until additional stone was piled around the tower and house at a later date. The photograph on page 292 shows the keeper's house as it looked around 1920.

In 1935 the lighthouse was automated, and the keeper's house was removed shortly thereafter, giving Portland Breakwater Light the appearance it has today (shown at right). During World War II, Portland Harbor was significantly developed to support the high-volume building of Liberty Ships. Once the shipyards were fully built out, the lighthouse was only 100 feet from shore, and because of the smaller breakwater, there was a lesser need for the lighthouse. In July of 1942, the light was extinguished as a wartime precaution and never relit.

The tower then sat undisturbed until 1990 when the Bicentennial Lighthouse Fund, the Maine Historic Preservation Commission, and the South Portland-Cape Elizabeth Rotary Club pooled efforts to raise $26,000 for structural repairs and painting. The sixth order Fresnel lens, which had been installed in the original 1855 tower but removed in 1993, was replaced with a modern 250mm optic in 2002, when the tower was renovated and the light relit.

The Portland Breakwater Light is now more commonly referred to as "Bug Light" by area residents. The site on which it sits is owned by the town of South Portland and is now part of a spacious new 8 acre park at the former East Yards shipbuilding complex. One of the great features of today's Bug Light Park is that it allows visitors to view the light close up. The park also has spectacular views of Portland Harbor and contains other interesting attractions, such as the replica Liberty ship exhibit shown on page 295. Portland Breakwater Light is one of our historical gems, and was added to the National Register of Historic Places on June 19, 1973.

A Ship on Way #5, South Portland Shipbuilding Corporation, 1943

So. Port. Ship. Corp. — West Div.
BLD #221
MCE #337
Keel 11-26-42
Way #5 — Feb. 20, 1943 — BOW

The New England Shipbuilding Corporation was a shipyard located near Portland Breakwater Light in the city of South Portland. The yard originated as two separate entities, the Todd-Bath Iron Shipbuilding Corporation and the South Portland Shipbuilding Corporation, which were created in 1940 and 1941 respectively, in order to meet the demand created by World War II. This photograph shows the bow of a ship on Way #5 at the West Division of the South Portland Shipbuilding Corporation on February 20, 1943. The ship became the John Trumbull. After the war, it was sold privately and scrapped in 1970.

The two yards merged in 1943, then continued to produce ships as the New England Shipbuilding Corporation's East Yard and West Yard. Both closed at the end of the war. The two yards built 266 ships: 154 in the East Yard, 112 in the West Yard. The first 30 East Yard ships were *Ocean* class cargo ships built for the United Kingdom. The remaining ships were of the Liberty Ship design, derived from the *Ocean* class, and were built for the United States Maritime Commission. To commemorate the achievement, the hull of a replica Liberty Ship, shown above, now forms the centerpiece of an exhibit at Bug Light Park.

Portland Head Light Around 1890

At the time construction began on the lighthouse at Portland Head in 1787, Maine was still a part of Massachusetts, whose legislature appropriated funds to begin the project. George Washington engaged two masons from Portland, Jonathan Bryant and John Nichols, to take charge of the construction and advised them that the colonial government was poor and to use materials from local fields and shores. The old tower, built of rubblestone, still stands as one of the four colonial lighthouses that have never been rebuilt. While under construction, the federal government was formed (in 1789) and the first congress authorized Alexander Hamilton in 1790 to inform the mechanics that they could go on to complete the tower. It was first lighted on January 10, 1791 with 16 lamps of whale oil.

Symbolizing the rockbound coast of Maine, the lighthouse at Portland Head, officially designated Portland Head Light, has aided mariners for over 200 years. Interestingly, the tower's height was changed several times. When Halfway Rock Light was built, Portland Head Light was considered less important and in 1833 the tower was shortened 20 feet. Mariners complained, however, and its height was restored in 1835. During the Civil War, raids on shipping became commonplace, and because of the necessity for ships at sea to sight Portland Head Light as soon as possible, the tower was raised eight feet. The current keeper's house, shown above, was built in 1891. Today, Portland Head Light is recognized as one of the most widely photographed lighthouses in the world.

Spurwink Meetinghouse, Cape Elizabeth – Then and Now

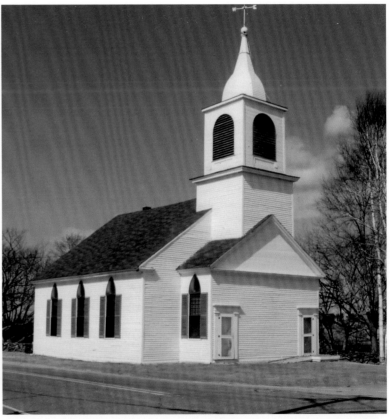

Overlooking the peaceful Riverside Cemetery and the marshes of the Spurwink River, not far from the original 1630 home site of George Cleeve on Richmond Island, the Spurwink Meetinghouse has stood its ground in Cape Elizabeth since 1802 as the oldest meetinghouse in town. With its blend of Federal, Gothic and Greek Revival styles, it is a simple structure with a sparse Puritan dé cor. In Cape Elizabeth, it is known affectionately as "the church of the holy oil can" because of the resemblance of its round, pointed cupola to a common oil can. Closed since 1957 for regular services but still open by reservation for weddings, funerals, and christenings, it is now owned by the Town of Cape Elizabeth. Within the grounds of the church everything becomes still, and among the gravestones the view down and across the winding marshlands is rugged and breathtaking. An air of calm and peace descends upon those who choose to enter here, and a timeless feeling surrounds this tiny part of the New England landscape. The meetinghouse was named to the National Register of Historic Places in 1970.

Appendix

Left blank intentionally

Appendix A: Panoramic view of Portland from the Fidelity Building

This panoramic view of Portland shot from the top of the Fidelity Building in 2010 is greatly changed from when the building first opened one hundred years earlier in 1910. On the left we see the very modern looking One City Center complex. This was once an entire block of buildings known as the "Golden Triangle" that fell victim to the wrecker's ball in the go-go, urban renewal days of the 1960s, along with, in the distance, the new Key Bank Plaza complex on Middle Street, where for nearly a hundred years stood the famous Falmouth Hotel, built by J.B. Brown in 1867-68 as a demonstration of civic pride after the Great Fire of 1866 (see page 100 for more on the Falmouth Hotel). In the distance from left to right are Peaks, House and Cushing's Islands, often referred to as Longfellow's Islands after the poet, which he himself likened to the Hesperides, the three nymphs who tend a blissful garden in a far western corner of the world.

Appendix B: Policeman in a Signal Box on Monument Square Around 1935

Early traffic lights, like the one shown above in Schenectady, New York, contained as many as seven different colored lenses, and required an attendant because they were manually operated. This led to much confusion and many accidents. To help solve the problem, the Portland Police Department took a practical approach and erected signal boxes at key intersections throughout the city, such as here at Monument Square (shown at left). This photograph from about 1935 shows officer George Dennison in the box directing traffic around what was then a rotary in the square circling the Soldiers and Sailors Monument. Another box is visible in the photograph on page 12 at Congress Square. Notice, in the photograph at left, the Clapp Block in the background, built in 1924 when Asa Clapp's home was finally torn down (see Appendix O on page 189). Notice also how much nicer the building appeared in this photograph as compared to the present-day image shown on page 37. Today, the windows in particular stand out as poor replacements for the originals.

Appendix C: A Tale of Four City Halls

 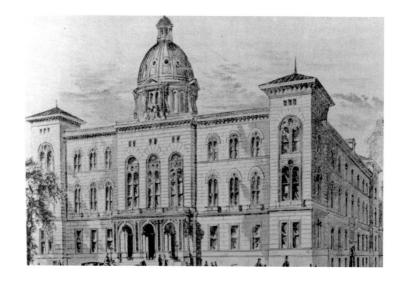

A Tale of Four City Halls. Top Left: Portland's first City Hall was originally built as a Market House at Market Square in 1825 to a design by John Kimball, Jr. (1783-1865), see Appendix Q on page 191 for the Market House, but redesigned into a City Hall in 1832 by Charles Quincy Clapp. He removed the tower and added some columns in the front to give it a Greek Revival look, shown here. Top right: The second City Hall was built between 1858 and 1864 at the head of Myrtle Street, but it didn't last long, as it was destroyed in the Great Fire of 1866. Lower left: The third City Hall was built on the same footprint as the second one; though city officials wanted it at Lincoln Park, the voters turned that idea down, insisting that it remain on Myrtle Street. It too burned in January 1908. Lower right: Our fourth City Hall was built in 1909-12 of granite from North Jay, and was designed by Carrere and Hastings of New York.

Appendix D: Portland High School in 1829

An early Portland High School (on the right) shown at the corner of Oak and Spring Streets around 1829 in a drawing by John Calvin Stevens.

Some accounts of the history of education in the United States use 1829 as the date of the origin of today's Portland High School. In that year, it was decided to divide secondary education in Portland into two schools, a Latin High School and an English High School. The Latin High School continued to emphasize the classical curriculum, which was mainly aimed at preparing boys for college. The English High School represented the new idea in public education with its main aim of preparing boys for "practical life activities." Included in this curriculum were reading, spelling, writing, arithmetic, geography, English grammar, composition, history, algebra, geometry, trigonometry, surveying, bookkeeping, natural philosophy, astronomy, and chemistry. The twin high schools established in 1829 were located in a building on the west corner of Oak and Spring Streets. This picture, showing the high school (on the right) and a next door grammar school (on the left), was sketched many years later by John Calvin Stevens. The twin school arrangement lasted only a few years. Attendance at the Latin High School dwindled and was closed in 1832, the partition between the two schools was removed, and the English High School became the only high school in Portland. The classical curriculum of the now defunct Latin High School was brought to the English High School, and from the mid-1830s the English High School prepared both the scholar desiring to go on to college and the student entering the world of business. The location of the school was changed again in 1845. In that year, it was moved next door into the former grammar school, where it remained until 1863 when the Cumberland Avenue school was opened.

Appendix E: The John J. Brown House on Spring Street

The Gothic Revival style reached the United States in the 1840s, but began in England almost a century earlier with Horace Walpole's remodeling of Strawberry Hill into a Gothic country house. Portland architect Henry Rowe (1810-1870) had English training, and he used it to full advantage in designing the stunning John J. Brown House in 1845. This home, a rare and superlative example of Gothic Revival architecture, was originally located at 86 Spring Street (shown at left), but was due to be demolished in 1971 to make room for the Holiday Inn that now occupies that site. Greater Portland Landmarks acquired the building, and in a superhuman effort involving the entire community, moved the home to its present location at 387 Spring Street (shown above). The home is constructed of wood, but made to look like stone; the corners are marked by applied decorative "pier buttresses" but the building retains the four-square central plan scheme of its classical predecessors. The entrance has been pulled out into a strong projecting pavilion, allowing for a steeply pointing gable and a charming porch. The hipped portion of the roof with its fish scale-patterned slate is accordingly tall, lending to this cottage some of the much admired soaring qualities of Gothic church architecture. This is the only home of its type in Maine, and one of the few to be found anywhere in the world.

Appendix F: The Portland Yacht Club designed by John Calvin Stevens in 1927

The beautiful thing about a John Calvin Stevens-designed building is how immediately recognizable it is. Call it what you want, but there is definitely something very "Stevensesque" about this, the second Portland Yacht Club, built at the end of Central Wharf in 1927 after the original 1885 building shown on page 80 had burned. Stevens was a yacht club member who enjoyed boating and the camaraderie of close friends. When the old club house burned, he came up with the design for the new one, shown here. The building served for 20 years until after World War II, when the Portland Yacht Club heard about a private summer residence in Falmouth Foreside that was coming on the market, and that might be able to be purchased and converted to a new clubhouse there on the Falmouth shore, which by then was deemed superior to the waterfront location in Portland.. Arrangements were made, the Falmouth property was purchased, and the Portland Yacht Club moved to its new location in Falmouth Foreside in 1947, where it has been ever since. When the subject of the "old" Portland Yacht Club comes up in conversation, this John Calvin Stevens-designed building of 1927 is the one that most people still alive remember seeing.

Appendix G: The Bramhall Estate of John Bundy Brown

Before Thornhurst, before the gaggle of red brick, Colonial Revival, John Calvin Stevens-designed mansions of Brown and Clifford family heirs clustered along Bowdoin and Vaughan Streets, and a century before the modernist Payson House in Falmouth, Bramhall was the magnificent private estate of Portland sugar baron John Bundy Brown (1805-1881). Built between 1855 and 1858 on a ten-acre lot on the Western Promenade, the home was designed by Charles A. Alexander (1822-1882), who had provided many of the designs for Portland's most beautiful Victorian mansions, including the H.J. Libby double house of 1852-53 (see page 12) and the Andrew and Samuel Spring Mansions of 1855. This would be no exception. John B. Brown was the son of Titus Olcott (1764-1855) and Susannah (Bundy) Brown (1771-1851) of Lancaster, New Hampshire, who had moved to Gray, Maine and married Ann Matilda Greely in 1830. Their children were Philip Henry (1831-1893), James Olcott (1836-1864), John Marshall (1838-1907), and Ellen Greely (1841-1904). Brown's was a classic rags to riches story, rising from a $50 a year grocery clerk in the firm of Shaw, Hammond and Carney to become Portland's leading capitalist and largest landowner. His estate was constructed on the profits of half a dozen successful ventures, including real estate and an immense sugar refinery on the Portland waterfront, and was one of the most imposing residences of the time. Brown also assembled a notable painting collection of American and European art, and filled the conservatory attached to his villa with sculpture, leaving the building open to the public for several days of the week. Upon his death in 1881, his vast collection of art was given to the Portland Museum of Art, where it can be seen to this day. As for Bramhall, it was regrettably demolished by his family in 1915.

Appendix H: The Demolition of Portland's Union Station

The date is August 31, 1961. It is a hot summer day as a crowd of onlookers gathers on St. John Street to witness the final destruction of Portland's magnificent Union Station. No laws have been broken, but people stand around and watch, as if helpless, as the clock tower comes crashing to the ground. Souvenir hunters would gather up pieces of granite, glass, and metal to take home with them as reminders of the fateful day. Suddenly the old station was gone, forever. The loss of Union Station left a deep and lasting wound in the architectural consciousness of the city, and heralded the beginning of the historic preservation movement.

Appendix I: General John Marshall Brown's Thornhurst Estate in Falmouth

General John Marshall Brown (1838-1907) was the third son of John Bundy and Ann Matilda (Greely) Brown. He lived in Portland after his return from the Civil War, but later became impressed with the future value of Falmouth Foreside and bought a large tract of land near Waite's Landing, where his home was. He was a great lover of agriculture and for years conducted large farming operations there on a scale that marked him as a successful gentleman farmer. General Brown had traveled extensively in England and he was imbued somewhat with the English idea of large landed estates, and his place at Falmouth was conducted much on the same basis. The farm maintained a herd of Jersey cows, many owned by other people, and the milk from each family's cows was delivered to that family. Shown above is the imposing three-story, 22-room summer "cottage", built around 1871, and designed for General Brown and his wife Alida Catherine Carroll (1844-1911) by an unknown architect. In 1882, Brown commissioned Francis H. Fassett and John Calvin Stevens to enlarge and remodel the cottage, complete with a center atrium, five fireplaces, oriel windows, a large porch, and an octagonal Tea House near the shore. Here the Browns lived with their five children: Sally Carroll (1867-1948), Alida Greely (1870-1889), Mary Brewster Derby (1876-), Carroll (1881-1960), and Violetta Lansdale Berry (1883-1971). In 1893, Brown's oldest daughter Sally Carroll married banker Herbert Payson (1860-1940), and that couple had six children: Alida Payson Snow (1895-1961), Anne Carroll Payson Holt (1896-1976), John Brown (1897-1945?), Charles Shipman (1898-1985), Herbert Jr. (1902-1967) and Olcott Sprigg (1907-1942). In 1926, Brown's grandson Herbert Payson, Jr. married Eileen McHenry (1903-1996), and by 1952 this couple had inherited the property. The first thing they did was tear it down, all except for the octagonal Tea House, designed by John Calvin Stevens, and still standing to this day (*see page 185*).

Appendix J: The Choragic Monument of Lysicrates

The Choragic Monument of Lysicrates near the Acropolis of Athens was erected by the *choregos* Lysicrates, a very wealthy citizen of ancient Athens and patron of many theatrical performances in the Theater of Dionysus, to commemorate the award of first prize in 334 B.C. to one of the performances he had sponsored. The *choregos* was the sponsor who paid for and supervised the training of the dramatic dance-chorus, a common practice by rich people of that time. In memory of this honor, Lysicrates financed and built the monument, shown at right as it looks today.

The monument is significant because the circular structure, raised on a high squared podium, is one of the first Greek monuments built according to the Corinthian order. Its frieze sculptures depict episodes from the myth of Dionysus, the god whose rites developed into Greek theater. It originally served as support for the bronze tripod that was given as a prize. It stands now in its little garden on the Tripodon Street ("Street of the Tripods"), which follows the line of the ancient street of the name, which led to the Theater of Dionysus and was once lined with choragic monuments.

By 1658, a French Capuchin monastery was founded on the site, and the monastery succeeded in purchasing the monument from the Turks in 1669. The monument became famous in France and England through engravings of it (like the one shown above center in *The Antiquities of Athens,* 1762), and "improved" versions became eye catching features in several English landscape gardens. Lord Byron stayed at the monastery during his second visit to Greece and wrote part of Childe Harold while in residence. In 1818, Friar Francis planted in its gardens the first tomato plants in Greece. The monastery was demolished during the Greek war of Independence in 1821. French archaeologists cleared the rubble from the half-buried monument and searched the area for missing architectural parts. In 1876, the architects Francois Boulanger and E. Levoit supervised a restoration under the auspices of the French government.

Famous British versions of the Choragic Monument are to be found in the gardens at Shugborough, Staffordshire, and on the tower of St. Giles Church in Elgin, among many others. In the U.S., the Choragic Monument was adapted for Civil War memorials, and capped many Beaux-Arts towers. It was also copied as a cupola atop the Tennessee State Capitol building. The design of Portland Breakwater Light was inspired by the monument. Shown above left is the original *wooden* Portland Breakwater Light, built in 1855, and replaced by the present cast-iron light designed by Thomas U. Walter in 1872.

Appendix K: The Modernist Payson Estate and the Octagonal Tea House

By 1952, Thornhurst had become a white elephant, too big for Brown family heir Herbert Payson Jr. and his wife Eileen to heat and maintain, so they had the mansion bulldozed, replacing it with a dwelling so modest and uncomplicated that one can't help but wonder if the massive, highly appointed original had provoked in the couple a reactionary streak. If nothing else, they were certainly bold, for the Payson House was decidedly cutting edge in 1952, and on the staid, traditional Foreside, it still seems so today. Shown above left, the Payson House is one of a handful of residences designed by the pioneering architect and artist Serge Chermayeff (1900-96). The Payson's son Michael was a roommate at the time at Phillips Academy in Andover with the architect's son, Ivan Chermayeff, now a distinguished designer responsible for many well known corporate logos such as NBC's peacock, and it was through the boys' friendship that the elder Paysons met the Russian-born, English-educated Serge. With its flat roof, boxlike structure and vertical gray wood siding broken by large expanses of glass, the Payson House is classic International Style, one of only a few such architect-designed houses in Maine. International Style is the American form of Bauhaus design, a school founded in Germany by architect Walter Gropius after World War I. The Bauhaus approach rejects cornices, eaves, rounded corners and other decorative details in favor of smooth facades, open floor plans and right angles. Chermayeff, who attracted the world's attention in 1935 when he designed with Eric Mendelsohn one of the United Kingdom's first modernist public buildings, the De La Warr Pavilion, was teaching at MIT when the Paysons commissioned him to build their house. "It was somewhat controversial," said Michael, who was 20 at the time. Extended family members, many of whom lived nearby on parcels that once comprised the Thornhurst Estate, didn't want to see the mansion razed. "I think they thought we were pretty crazy to have this sort of place, but over the years they came to like it." It's clear there were moments of great doubt once construction began. Eileen Payson noted in a journal she kept in 1952 as her family was just moving in: "Comments of all sorts whirled around us, some of it favorable, some critical, until one young friend suggested that we hang a sign on the front door saying simply, 'We don't like your house either.'" And finally, stating a truth that continues to this day in the house, Mrs. Payson noted: "Now the house is completed. It looks lovely, and it hugs the landscape with affection. Our own part in this creative experience is about to begin. We are gong to live there." Today, the Payson House is home to Herbert and Eileen Payson's son, Michael, and his wife, Barbara. From their living room in summer they can see the forest of sailboat masts at Handy Boat Marina and the Portland Yacht Club, including the original octagonal Tea House designed by Stevens at the edge of the shore (shown above right). In winter when the snow is falling, this same room is "like being inside a paperweight," said Michael. "In winter I am transfixed," Barbara agreed. "I like feeling part of nature." Fifty-eight years after it was built, the Payson House has become a landmark in itself, and is now listed on the National Register of Historic Places.

Appendix L: Leon Leonwood Bean

Leon Leonwood Bean (1872-1967) was forty years old when he started his company, working out of the basement of his brother's apparel shop. He didn't even have a store yet, but he did have a revolutionary idea of how to solve the problem of cold, damp feet that plagued hunters. L.L. enlisted a local cobbler to stitch leather uppers to workmen's rubber boots, creating a comfortable, functional boot for exploring the Maine woods. This innovative boot – the Maine Hunting Shoe – changed outdoor footwear forever and began one of the most successful family-run businesses in the country.

L.L. did not meet with immediate success. The rubber bottoms separated from the leather tops, and 90 of the first 100 pairs he had sold were returned. Although it nearly put him out of business, L.L. kept his word and refunded the purchase price. He borrowed more money, corrected the problem and, with undiminished confidence, mailed more brochures. L.L. had learned the value of personally testing his products, of honest advertising based on firm convictions and of keeping the customer satisfied at any cost. These were lessons that would serve him well in the coming years.

With the growing success of the Maine Hunting Shoe, L.L. Bean began to develop rugged, comfortable clothing to wear in the outdoors. The fact that he was an outdoorsman who not only developed and tested his products, but also guaranteed them to be 100% satisfactory in every way, established him as one of the most respected names in the business. He ran his company until his death at the age of 94 on February 5, 1967. He attributed his long life and good health to the time he spent in the outdoors.

The company L.L. Bean started has been a trusted source for quality apparel, reliable outdoor equipment and expert advice since 1912. It is headquartered in Freeport, Maine, just down the road from the original store. The company has now grown from a one-man operation to a global organization with annual sales in excess of $1.5 billion.

His is a true American success story!

Appendix M: John Calvin Stevens

John Calvin Stevens
(1855-1940)

No book on the history of Portland would be complete without some mention of the architect John Calvin Stevens (1855-1940). Anyone researching her history does not get very far along before running into him, as he designed more than 300 buildings in Portland alone over a nearly 70-year-long period.

John Calvin Stevens was a prolific and innovative architectural genius who moved to Portland from Boston with his family when he was two years old and lived here for over eighty years until his death in 1940. From the early 1880s to the 1930s, Stevens worked in a wide range of styles, from the Queen Anne and Romanesque popular at the beginning of his career, to the Arts and Crafts, Mission, and Prairie School designs of the 1920s. Some of his buildings show an eclectic mix of all these styles, but the architect is best known for his pioneering efforts in the Shingle and Colonial Revival styles, examples of which abound in this area.

Stevens gained a national audience for his work with the publication in 1889 of *Examples of American Domestic Architecture*, co-authored with his partner Albert Winslow Cobb. However, it was the publication after his death of Vincent Scully's *The Shingle Style* by Yale in 1955 that brought him international fame.

John Calvin Stevens is without a doubt one of Portland's most famous sons, second only perhaps to Henry Wadsworth Longfellow. His designs can be found all along the Maine coast, as well as in Portland and its suburbs. In recognition of his hundreds of buildings on the Portland peninsula, with dozens more in the surrounding neighborhoods and islands, the city declared October 8, 2009 to be John Calvin Stevens Day. The ceremony included a Congressional Record of Recognition presented by the Office of Senator Olympia Snowe.

Appendix N: Theodore Roosevelt visiting Thomas Brackett Reed at his home in Portland in 1902

People transform space into place. Physical geography and the built environment may shape our relationship to a place, but communities like Portland are also *storied* places. Their identities are shaped by the narratives we tell about the past. Often these stories and images structure how we perceive a particular locale, and define its significance and distinctiveness. Take this picture for example.

The right half of this brick double house at 32 Deering Street might have been anybody's home, but it wasn't. From 1888 until his death in 1902, U.S. Congressman Thomas Brackett Reed (1839-1902) lived here. Born in Portland in 1839, Reed served in the U.S. House from 1877 to 1899. He was Speaker of the House from 1889-91 and 1895 until his resignation in 1899. Known for his wit and his brilliant parliamentary ability, Reed was mentioned for the Republican nomination for President in 1892 and 1896, but was unsuccessful in obtaining it. When asked about his chances for receiving the nomination, he answered, "They could do worse, and they probably will." When a congressman said to him he'd rather be right than be President, Reed assured him, "Don't worry, you'll never be either." His social circle included intellectuals and politicians, from Theodore Roosevelt to Mark Twain.

Captured in this image, President Theodore Roosevelt (1858-1919) waves his hat to a crowd of well-wishers outside the home of his friend during a visit to Portland on August 26, 1902. Roosevelt was William McKinley's vice president (elected in 1900) and became president when McKinley was assassinated and died on September 14, 1901. Roosevelt spent two college summers in Maine (1878 and 1879) at Island Falls, camping, fishing, and exploring, and later wrote the essay "My Debt to Maine" about his experiences there.

Images like this one remind us that Portland is both a place on the ground and a territory of the imagination, a lived experience as well as a mental landscape. By documenting the city's richly textured history, such images create a narrative sense of place, and for the many thousands of us who are fortunate to live here, that place is the place we call home.

Appendix O: The Asa Clapp Mansion

Asa Clapp (1762-1848) was somewhat of an enigma. One of Portland's wealthiest men, he made a multi-million loan – fully half his fortune - to the federal government to help finance the War of 1812. Shortly thereafter, he enlisted as a private in the Portland militia at the age of 50, humbly assuming his position among the rank and file of farmers and fishermen. In 1799, Clapp joined Captain Joseph McLellan and his son Major Hugh McLellan in founding the Portland Bank, but Hugh McLellan's business habits did not appeal to Clapp. He resigned and signed on with James Deering, Matthew "King" Cobb and others to found the Maine Bank, igniting a war of one-upsmanship among the leaders of Portland's elite. This rivalry was measured by the size and grandeur of the homes they acquired. In 1804, Clapp bought the two-story Daniel Davis house and commissioned Alexander Parris (1780-1852) to turn it into a Federal Period mansion, shown above. Parris's many improvements, including a circular staircase lighted by an octagonal cupola, and the imposing size of the now-three-story house, turned it into one of the city's premier showplaces. In later life, Clapp was visited there by Presidents Monroe, Polk and Buchannan.

Appendix P: The Three Johns

John Alfred Poor

(1808-1871)

John Bundy Brown
(1805-1881)

John Calvin Stevens
(1855-1940)

Portland's three eminent Johns have deservedly received much historical attention. John Alfred Poor, John Bundy Brown, and John Calvin Stevens did much to make Portland the great city that she is. In fact, try to imagine what the city would be like without the imprint of these men. What if they had never lived?

John Alfred Poor was responsible for Portland becoming the terminus of the Atlantic and St. Lawrence Railroad. In an era when shipbuilding was at its peak, Poor understood that railroads held the key to Maine's economic future. He abandoned his Bangor law practice and generated the idea that Portland, with her magnificent harbor, should be linked by rail with Montreal and become Canada's winter sea outlet. His untiring efforts paid off when, on February 10, 1845, the Canadian government issued a charter to Portland for the building of a railroad connecting it to Montreal. The Atlantic and St. Lawrence Railroad, later taken over by the Grand Trunk, brought carloads of grain to Portland from Canada for reshipment. The prosperity it brought to Portland exceeded even John Poor's dreams. By 1872, there were sixty-five trains a day stopping in Portland, which aided the city's ability to become a major center for exportation. Poor's enthusiasm for railroads also extended to building his own locomotives, and in 1847 he established the Portland Company, which developed a national reputation for constructing locomotives, boilers, and other machinery. Without John Poor's influence, none of this would have happened.

John Bundy Brown came to Portland as a fifty-dollar a year clerk in Alpheus Shaw's grocery store on Middle Street, and through perseverance and ability became Portland's leading capitalist. With interests in banking, railroads, and real estate, he became the city's larges landowner. In 1855, Brown formed the Portland Sugar Company, which produced 250 barrels of sugar per day and earned over half a million dollars per year. (See Appendix G on page 181 for more.)

John Calvin Stevens was a prolific and inventive architectural genius who designed more than 300 buildings in Portland alone. An originator of the Shingle Style of architecture, his designs can be found all along the Maine coast, as well as in Portland and its suburbs. In recognition of his hundreds of buildings on the Portland peninsula, the city declared October 8, 2009 to be John Calvin Stevens Day. (For more on John Calvin Stevens, see Appendix M on page 187.)

Appendix Q: The Saga of the Cupola from the Market House or Old City Hall

ALUMNI HALL, WESTBROOK JUNIOR COLLEGE, PORTLAND, MAINE

This is everything you always wanted to know about the cupola from the Market House or Old City Hall at Monument Square. Top left: A drawing by Charles Goodhue of the original Market House as it looked when first built in 1825. The original John Kimball, Jr. (1783-1865) design was modified by Charles Clapp in 1832 into Portland's first City Hall. The ground floor of the building had stalls for selling produce, with a hall for militia training above. Top right: The Market House as remodeled by Charles Quincy Clapp (1799-1868) shows the addition of a columned portico and removal of the cupola, transforming the building into the more massive and severe Greek Revival style. Though few examples remain, this "temple" style of Greek Revival architecture was once an important visual factor in the Portland scene (see, for example, the Exchange on page 193.) Bottom left: Alumni Hall at Westbrook Junior College was built in 1834, and used the unwanted cupola removed from the Market House two years earlier. Bottom right: Alumni Hall as it looks today, with the cupola still very much intact.

Appendix R: The Matthew Cobb Mansion

In 1800, the young architect Alexander Parris (1780-1852) and his new bride Silvina Bonney Stetson moved from Massachusetts to Portland, Maine, which was then experiencing a building boom. The Royal Navy had bombarded the city during the Revolution, reducing three-quarters of it to ashes in 1775. But following the war, its trade recovered, almost challenging Boston as the busiest port in New England, and Parris received numerous residential and commercial commissions here, including one, in 1801, to design a new home for the wealthy merchant Matthew "King" Cobb . Cobb (1752-1824) was partners with Asa Clapp, James Deering and others in founding the Maine Bank, and was easily the city's highest taxpayer. Of this frame style home, whose boards were laid flush, historian Nathan Goold's father, William, noted in 1816: "Its unsullied white front, with no sign of joint or seam, gave it the appearance of being cut from an immense block of statuary marble, leaving the carved ornaments standing out in relief." After nearly a century of use, the home was demolished in 1898 to make way for the new Y.M.C.A. building, which later became known as the Libby Building. The Libby Building itself was demolished when the Payson wing of the Portland Museum of Art opened in 1983. Charles Shipman Payson (1898-1985), a son of Portland banker Herbert Payson (1860-1940) and Sally Carroll Brown (1867-1948), had married Joan Whitney (1903-1975), owner of the New York Mets and daughter of sports tycoon Payne Whitney. She inherited a trust fund from her grandfather, William C. Whitney, and on her father's passing in 1927, received a large part of her family fortune. Charles Shipman Payson donated 17 paintings by Winslow Homer and $8 million to construct the building in which they would be housed. It is perhaps an ironic twist of fate that the architect for the Payson wing was Henry Nichols Cobb (1926-), a founding principal of I.M. Pei & Partners, and a direct descendant of Matthew "King" Cobb. According to Mr. Cobb, the design of the building sought "to respect and render eloquent the living presence of history on and around the Museum site." The Cobb Mansion on Congress Square is shown here as it looked around 1890. Notice also the second building on the right past the church. This is the former Stephen McLellan Mansion, home to the Cumberland Club since 1895, and still standing today.

Appendix S: The Merchant's Exchange, corner of Middle and Exchange Streets

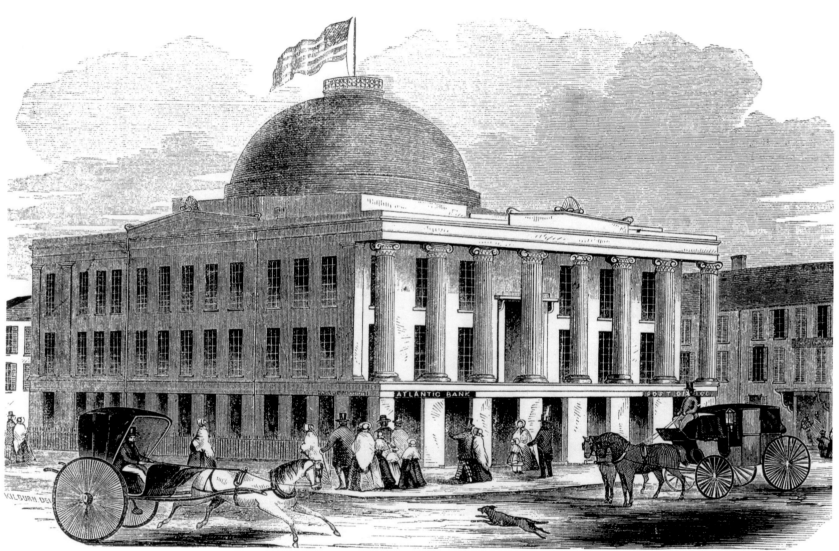

Although few examples remain, the "temple" style of Greek Revival architecture was once an important visual factor in the Portland scene. The Old City Hall in Market Square was one (see pages 177 and 191); the Exchange Building was another. The Merchant's Exchange was built between 1836 and 1839, and burned only fifteen years later in 1854. It once stood at Middle and Exchange Streets where the Old Post Office was later built between 1868 and 1871. Designed by the prominent Boston architect Richard Bond (1797-1861), its 72 foot façade consisted of a high basement story supporting a two story Ionic colonnade. The length on Exchange Street was 136 feet and the whole was surmounted by a shallow dome 63 feet in diameter. If modern-day Portlanders lament the loss of Union Station from nothing more than their own apathy, imagine how 19th century citizens felt when this architectural masterpiece burned to the ground by accident.

Appendix T: Aerial View of Maine Medical Center and West End

Maine Medical Center is a 637-bed teaching hospital, and the largest tertiary care facility in Northern New England, serving all of Maine and parts of Vermont and New Hampshire. The present-day complex of more than one million square feet was completed in 1984. In 2009, Maine Medical Center completed a major expansion, including a new and improved emergency department, birthing center, neonatal intensive care unit, helipad, utility plant, and parking garage. A million square feet is a lot of space, and to truly appreciate the size of the complex requires an aerial photograph, like this one. Running along the bottom of the picture is St. John Street, where Union Station was once located, while at left is Park Avenue leading to Deering Oaks Park. Congress Street can be seen winding its way up the hill just to the left of the hospital complex. The old Maine General Building of 1874 is still visible at the heart of the complex, but just barely. Portland's peninsula geography is especially evident in this photograph, with downtown and Munjoy Hill in the distance, and the islands of Casco Bay beyond.

Index

Index

Index

Index

Illustration Credits

Unless otherwise noted, all contemporary images were photographed by the author. The remaining illustrations and photographs are credited as follows:

From the author's collection: * Page 2: Map of Ancient Falmouth * Page 16: Electric trolleys * Page 78: Aerial view of East End * Page 120: Union Station * Page 162: Town Landing Market * Page 176 (right) Traffic light * Page 178: Portland High School * Page 180: Portland Yacht Club * Page 181: Bramhall Estate * Page 182: Union Station * Page 183: Thornhurst * Page 184: (all) Choragic Monument of Lysicrates * Page 185: Payson Home and Tea House * Page 186: Leon Leonwood Bean * Page 190 (all) John Poor, John Brown, John Stevens * Page 193: Merchant's Exchange *

Collections of the Maine Historical Society: * Page 6 (right) Monument Square * Page 12: H.J. Libby House * Page 14: Rines Brothers Company * Page 34: Preble Mansion * Page 36: Asa Clapp House * Page 46: Goodhue drawing of Munjoy Hill * Page 58: Grand Army of the Republic * Page 60: Fourth of July * Page 62: Portland Company cars * Page 66: Two women in car * Page 68: Two men in car * Page 70: North School * Page 76: Abyssinian Church * Page 90: Board of Trade * Page 98: Oxen in front of Seamen's Club * Page 105: West End * Page 106: Henley Kimball * Page 108: Columbia Market * Page 110: Deering Estate * Page 112: Gas station on Forest Avenue * Page 116: Forest City Chevrolet * Page 138: Veteran's Memorial Bridge * Page 160: Bramhall columns * Page 168: Ship on Way #5 * Page176 (left): Signal box * Page 187: John Calvin Stevens * Page 188: Theodore Roosevelt * Page 192: Cobb Mansion.

Courtesy of the Maine Historic Preservation Commission: * Page 6 (left): Monument Square * Page 8: Two boys and air mail wagon * Page 11: Panoramic view of Downtown * Page 18: Deering Block * Page 20: Preble Street * Page 22: Congress Square * Page 24: High Street * Page 26: Eastland Hotel * Page 28: Lower Hays * Page 30: City Hall * Page 32: Longfellow Square * Page 38: Forest Avenue * Page 40: Portland High School * Page 42: Chestnut Street Methodist Church * Page 44: Monument Square * Page 45: E.P. Quinn * Page 48: Morning Street * Page 50: Portland Company * Page 52: Longfellow birthplace * Page 54: Portland Observatory * Page 64: Grand Trunk terminal * Page 72: St. Paul's Anglican Church * Page 74: St. Lawrence Church * Page 79: Hannaford Brothers Company * Page 80: Portland Yacht Club * Page 82: Swasey Company * Page 84: Old Post Office * Page 86: Upper Exchange Street * Page 88: Curtis Company * Page 92: Rich Printers * Page 94: Exchange Street * Page 96: Boothby Square * Page 100: Falmouth Hotel * Page 102: Custom House * Page 104: Berry Printers * Page 114: Huston Biscuit Company * Page 118: Portland Municipal Airport * Page 122: Union Station * Page 124: Read Street * Page 126: Forest City Diner * Page 128: Cobblestones at Bramhall Square * Page 130: Maine General Hospital * Page 132: Union Station * Page 133: Million Dollar Bridge * Page 134: Tukey's Bridge * Page 136: Vaughan's Bridge * Page 140: Baxter Boulevard * Page 142: Fort Allen * Page 144: Western Promenade * Page 146: Eastern Promenade * Page 148: Eastern Promenade * Page 150: Lincoln Park * Page 152: Deering Oaks * Page 154: Duck House * Page 156: Mansion in the Park * Page 158: Bandstand at Fort Allen * Page 159: Downtown Freeport * Page 164: Fort McKinley * Page 166: Portland Breakwater Light * Page 170: Portland Head Light * Page 172: Spurwink Meeting House * Page 177 (top left, top right, bottom left) City Hall * Page 189: Asa Clapp House * Page 191: (top left, top right, bottom left) Market House, City Hall, Alumni Hall. *

Courtesy of Greater Portland Landmarks: * Page 56: Entertainment of the Boston Rifle Rangers at the Portland Observatory (1830) * Page 179: John J. Brown House (both) *

Courtesy of Maine Medical Center: * Page194: Aerial view of Maine Medical Center *